PRAISE FOR
HOW TO BE A BETTER PERSON

"It's never too late to self-improve, and *How to Be a Better Person* makes it a joy to do so. Hanley's tips will get you moving your legs, mind, and point of view to a new place. This book is accessible and thought-provoking—just reading it made me happy!"

—Katy Bowman, author of *Move Your DNA*
and *Movement Matters*

"Simple without dumbing down and uplifting without bright-siding, *How to Be a Better Person* is a beautiful book for any of us who could use some guidance in the direction of having a life that feels more useful and nourishing and less fraught."

—Brooke Thomas, host of the podcasts
Liberated Body and *Bliss + Grit*

"I couldn't help smiling while reading Kate Hanley's book, imagining what the world would be like if we all followed this advice. We'd have less strife and anxiety, more connected relationships, and more purposeful lives. Simply put: we'd all be better people."

—Amy Gallo, author of *HBR Guide to
Dealing with Conflict*

"What an incredible amount of life wisdom is contained in this well-laid-out and easy-to-read book! In *How to Be a Better Person*, each of Kate Hanley's tips gives us opportunity for pause, inquiry, and action in an otherwise busy world. You will come out of this book feeling your personal best, ready to make a difference!"

—Amy Jen Su, coauthor of *Own the Room: Discover Your Signature Voice to Master Your Leadership Presence*

"If you're wondering how you can be a better person and make the world a better place, take this book home with you, keep it by your bedside table, and dip into it whenever you need inspiration. By sharing these practical strategies and mindset shifts, Kate Hanley offers just the loving kick in the pants we all sometimes need to make the difference we know deep down we were put here to make."

—Lisa Sasevich, The Queen of Sales Conversion

400+ SIMPLE WAYS TO MAKE A DIFFERENCE IN YOURSELF—AND THE WORLD

HOW TO BE A

Better

Person

Kate Hanley

Adams Media
New York   London   Toronto   Sydney   New Delhi

Aadamsmedia
Adams Media
An Imprint of Simon & Schuster, Inc.
57 Littlefield Street
Avon, Massachusetts 02322

First Adams Media trade paperback edition DECEMBER 2017

ADAMS MEDIA and colophon are trademarks of Simon and Schuster.

For information about special discounts for bulk purchases, please contact Simon & Schuster Special Sales at 1-866-506-1949 or business@simonandschuster.com.

The Simon & Schuster Speakers Bureau can bring authors to your live event. For more information or to book an event contact the Simon & Schuster Speakers Bureau at 1-866-248-3049 or visit our website at www.simonspeakers.com.

Interior design by Sylvia McArdle and Colleen Cunningham
Interior images by Sylvia McArdle

Manufactured in the United States of America

10 9 8 7 6 5 4 3 2 1

Library of Congress Cataloging-in-Publication Data
Hanley, Kate.
How to be a better person / Kate Hanley.
Avon, Massachusetts: Adams Media, 2017.
LCCN 2017035848 (print) | LCCN 2017037528 (ebook) | ISBN 9781507205266 (pb) | ISBN 9781507205273 (ebook)
LCSH: Self-actualization (Psychology) | Happiness. | Motivation (Psychology) | BISAC: SELF-HELP / Personal Growth / Happiness. | SELF-HELP / Motivational & Inspirational. | SELF-HELP / Personal Growth / General.
LCC BF637.S4 (ebook) | LCC BF637.S4 H3434 2017 (print) | DDC 170/.44--dc23
LC record available at https://lccn.loc.gov/2017035848

ISBN 978-1-5072-0526-6
ISBN 978-1-5072-0527-3 (ebook)

Contents

Introduction

In the mid-2010s, for the first time ever, the most popular New Year's resolution in America was to be a better person. Not to lose weight, quit smoking, or something else that has a focus on what we *don't* want. Rather, we are longing to move toward something we *do* want. And this something doesn't just benefit us as individuals—it also contributes to a better world.

It's a beautiful thing.

And yet, it can feel a little vague. What does being a better person even mean?

What it *doesn't* mean is that you need to morph yourself into a perfect person—you can still forget birthdays, say things you wish you hadn't said, or phone it in at work from time to time. It *does* mean making progress in a positive direction so that you become a better version of who you already are. You can still have quirks, but they'll distinguish rather than define you.

Some of that progress will be in areas that are easier to quantify—such as being healthy, letting go of stuff, giving back, and working well. Some of it involves improving softer skills—such as showing love, seeing the positive, and staying committed. All told, they are small steps that add up to a big change in how you feel about yourself, how you show up for others, and how you impact the world in general.

How do you get started?

On these pages are 401 specific things you can do to work on both the practical components of being a better person as well as the more philosophical aspects. Please resist the urge to see these 401 things as a giant to-do list—you absolutely do not have to master all of them. On the other hand, it's motivating to see some physical evidence of your progress—that's why there are check boxes next to each activity. When you read one of the activity suggestions in this book, such as "Come bearing gifts" or "Name your feelings" and realize, *Hey, I do that now*, check the box! It's a great feeling.

Whether your primary aim is to share a better you with the rest of the world or to develop your inner self, you'll find that self-improvement ripples across your entire life. This book returns again and again to this insight: when you become a better person, you'll see it and know it, and others will too.

To me, being a better person means being less reactive, more empathetic, and more courageous. It means being willing to do hard work and doing the right thing—and working on being better at discerning what that "right thing" is. And all the while, also being lighthearted and having fun. Only you know what "being a better person" means to you, though. So, the first thing you'll need to do is think about what is important to you and what your goals are. Then choose a handful of items you want to focus on for the next week or month. When you feel you've got those well in hand, choose a new batch. Writing down the items you want to work on, or checking them off here in this book, will help you remember what you're committing to.

There's a reason why there are so many ways to be a better person listed in this book—to convey the fact that there is no three-step formula you can just whiz through and be done. You're never truly "done," because being better is a moving target. Meaning, there will always be more good stuff available to you. And that's worth celebrating.

PART ONE

See the Positive

Being "better" starts in your own mind, because you can't create what you can't imagine. The first step, then, is to train yourself to see the good that's already there—in yourself, in other people, in situations (even those that might otherwise seem pretty crappy)— and to imagine new positive possibilities. When you can do that, it frees you up from negative thinking that may have been keeping you stuck in unhelpful patterns. After all, the word *better* requires something to change— otherwise, you'd just stay the same. Teaching yourself to see the positive helps you change the one thing you truly have power over—your own mind.

RETRAIN YOUR BRAIN TO FIND THE GOOD STUFF

The human brain is wired to look for threats—a trait that kept us alive when we were living on the savannas but that can prevent happiness in our modern lives. This so-called "negativity bias" can keep you focused on what's going wrong (which explains why complaining is such a popular pastime). To bust out of this neural rut, train yourself to acknowledge when things go *right*. If you keep a calendar or a journal, make a point to write down what went well. If you're more of a verbal processor, start your conversations with friends by sharing a recent win (anything that gives you that *yesssss* feeling). Where the mind goes, reality follows. The more you appreciate life, the more reasons you have to celebrate it.

LOOK FOR THE LOVING REASON

It's one thing to look back at the past and see the good that came out of any rough patches; it's a much rarer ability to trust that something you're currently experiencing is working out to your advantage. Apply the wisdom of hindsight to the present by looking for the possible positive developments a current situation may be helping to create. This isn't about wishful thinking—it's about trusting that life is happening *for* you, not *to* you.

◻ ASSUME THE BEST ABOUT OTHERS

You may know that to assume makes an "ass" out of "u" and "me," but are you aware of how many blanks you subconsciously fill in every day? Whenever you decide that the driver in front of you is an idiot or that your spouse's silence means he's mad, you mistake opinion for fact. If you assume instead that this driver is on the way to visit a relative in the hospital or your partner is just thinking about his day, you'll find yourself interacting with others in a kinder, more positive way. How else might you interpret the things you make snap judgments about? Other, more loving explanations exist—if you allow yourself to look for them.

◻ BE YOUR OWN COMPETITION

Comparison is the thief of joy because it's based on a belief that if someone else has more, it must mean there's less left for you. If you're going to compare yourself to anyone, let it be yourself from two days ago, or last week, or last year. Let yourself see how far you've come—that's the best motivation to keep going. Everyone else can do her own thing and reach her own heights—there's plenty of success to go around. Be your own friendly rival.

REFRAME YOUR LIFE STORY

Let's face it: we didn't all grow up well nourished, in any sense of the word. You may well have been on the wrong end of unfairness and injustice. And yet, every single thing you've experienced—good or bad—has helped forge your unique package of strengths, skills, wisdom, and perspective. If you moved a lot as a kid because your parents had a hard time finding stable work, for example, you have well-honed skills at being able to size up new environments and an outsider's perspective that may make you a great business consultant. Can you aim to view everything you've experienced thus far as a training ground hand-tailored to teach you everything you need to succeed? You have to come to terms with the hurts that are bound up in your story so that you don't continue to feel wounded by them (counseling and/or coaching can be very helpful with this). When you do, you'll start to see what you're on this planet to do—for both yourself and others—and to believe that you can do it.

GET CLEAR ON YOUR VALUES

A value is a trait or quality that you prize—you do have them, even if you're not always aware of them. Your values can be fantastic motivators and barometers of happiness and success. Knowing them and making choices that align with them can also draw others to you who share the same values, leading to deeper connections. It can be surprisingly challenging, however, to identify and express your values clearly and confidently. To unearth yours, think about the times you were happiest, proudest, and most fulfilled. What about those particular times was so satisfying? Write those themes down and keep the list somewhere handy. Referring to them the next time you're deciding on a course of action will likely help illuminate the connection between your values and the decision at hand, and will help lead you somewhere you'll be happy to be.

LEARN FROM OTHERS

Thinking that you already know everything you need to know about anything—or everything—keeps you from being curious and learning more. (And there is *always* more insight to be had.) If your mind were a cup, imagine that it always has room in it for more tea. You never know when an idea is going to come along and change your life, so keep some space open for new thinking.

PUT YOUR BAD HABITS
TO GOOD USE

Everyone has a quirk or two—a tendency to procrastinate, or to be messy—that may get better over time but never fully goes away. Channel those negative traits toward positive ends. For example, if you put off cleaning out the fridge, use that time to volunteer at the animal shelter instead. Or pour your messiness into expressive works of art. When you see your quirks not as a problem to be fixed but an energy to be harnessed, you'll find all kinds of ways to put them to good use.

SIGN YOUR WORK

Humility is often a virtue, but not when it's a form of hiding. An artist who doesn't sign her canvas leaves a big question mark in the minds of the viewers of her art—an uncertainty that can lessen the enjoyment of the work. When you do something you're proud of, take credit for it. Share a sincere post about it on social media, tell a friend or loved one about it, or raise your hand at the staff meeting when your manager asks if anyone has a status update. Even if you're not proud of it, own it, and know that signing your name will inspire you to do better next time.

BUILD YOUR CALLUSES

A pedicurist may disagree, but calluses are actually something to be proud of. They show that you've done some heavy lifting, or walked a tough road. When you're facing a challenging time, imagine that you are building resilience and be open to the potential for growth. During a tough breakup, for example, trust that all those times you start crying when someone casually asks "How are you?" will help you be more real with people even when you aren't heartbroken. Or, imagine that the time-management skills you have to develop during a crunch time at work will help you get more done with less stress when everything calms down. It doesn't mean you have to suffer your way through; it just means you can stop resisting and start trusting that you will be able to acclimate—and that those adaptations will serve you well in the future.

EMBRACE BOREDOM

Boredom might seem like a bad thing, but it's a much-needed counterpoint to information overload and vital to your long-term health, happiness, and productivity. To get more comfortable with boredom, build your ability to resist meaningless distraction. Whenever you think, *I'm bored*, lean into that feeling instead of instinctively reaching for the nearest gadget. Look around you. Find someone else with a free moment and talk. Wonder about something in your immediate environment, then return to the next item on your list with more focus.

CULTIVATE GRATITUDE

When you nourish something it grows, for better or worse. If you focus on the negative, it empowers negativity in your life. If you focus on gratitude, it encourages positive growth in your life. Make acknowledging your gratitude part of your daily routine—list it in your journal or planner, share it at the dinner table or during bedtime with the kids, repeat it to yourself as you lie in bed at night. Devote some attention to the things you're thankful for and you'll find more and more things to appreciate—and you'll probably notice a little more gratitude coming right back your way.

PLAY THE HERO

You may have faced more than your fair share of hardships, but seeing yourself as a victim and trying to make others feel sorry for you (whether or not you realize you're doing it) is disempowering—big time. Instead, congratulate yourself for surviving and forgive yourself for anything you had to do to survive. Seeing yourself as a plucky hero instead of a helpless victim helps you take back your power. Do it, and use your newfound heroism to create a happier story.

☐ PRACTICE PAYING ATTENTION

Mindfulness is paying attention to what's happening right now without judging whether it is good or bad. Practicing mindfulness is calming, because it shifts your focus away from stress-producing thoughts, but it is also energizing, because you stop scattering your mental energies in a million directions. Any time you feel anxious or stressed, bring your attention back to what's happening right now. In this very moment, what can you see and hear? What can you feel? Shut out everything else.

☐ EXAMINE YOUR BIASES

Biases are subconscious judgments that have solidified into beliefs and keep people disconnected from others and from reality. So, ask yourself who you judge. Slow drivers? Conservatives? Liberals? Working moms? Stay-at-home moms? Challenge yourself to list your prejudgments and ask yourself why you feel that way. Then look for ways your thinking might be flawed. Could there be a good reason that person drives slowly? We all make judgments and put others into boxes at times, and it takes a conscious effort to really see our subtler biases, but challenging the stereotypes you've taken for granted will make you a more compassionate person.

☐ SEE THE MANY SHADES OF GRAY

Humans love to put things into black-and-white categories—good or bad, right or wrong—when in most cases there's a whole spectrum of possibility between these poles. Often, there is no one right answer. It may seem like you have to get the advanced degree *before* you can pursue the new career, for example, but there's likely some way you can start working or volunteering in that area now to ensure you actually like it before you make the jump. Let go of the need to be correct and see the many options available to you at any turn. If you knew you couldn't be wrong, that whatever you chose to do next would be okay, what would you do?

☐ TAKE SOME OF THE FEAR OUT OF CHANGE

Change is the one true constant in life and while it can be scary, it's always an opportunity for growth. And you were born to grow and evolve. When your life is changing, whether you're instigating the shift or it's being thrust upon you, two great mantras to use are *I embrace change*, which helps you accept the uncertainty instead of resist it, and *This or something better*, which helps keep your attention on possibility instead of loss.

☐ SAVE BEING SAFE FOR BASEBALL

A desire to stay safe often colors many life decisions—whether you want to move to a new city for that exciting-sounding job, for example, or if you should walk over and introduce yourself to that person at the party who seems like someone you'd like to get to know. But the truth is there is no such thing as 100 percent safe (unless you're playing baseball). No one knows what will happen next. You may decide not to move, but then the company you work for unexpectedly goes out of business. The good news is that the opposite of a truth is also true—if there is no safe, there's also no unsafe, particularly when you are following the deeper desires of your heart. So make the choice that's calling to you and leave the worrying about what's safe and what's not to the umpires.

☐ KNOW WHEN TO GIVE IT A REST

Weighing your options is great, but overanalyzing is just a waste of time and energy—and when you hit this stage, on some level you know it. It contributes to anxiety and relies too heavily on the cognitive mind. The ability to reason is important, but it is just one aspect of human intelligence. You also have wisdom and intuition, but it's hard to hear them if you're consumed with running the numbers and making pro and con lists.

☐ # MAKE NO EXCUSES

When you make excuses, you're subtly (or not so subtly) trying to wiggle out of responsibility. For one day, vow not to make excuses. If something doesn't go the way you planned, don't go into a story about it. Simply say, "This didn't go the way I'd planned but here's what I'm going to do about it." The person on the other end of the letdown will appreciate that you're taking responsibility instead of making excuses. Be the creator in your life, not the victim.

☐ # REFUSE TO COMPLAIN

No one likes to hear a litany of complaints, no matter how justified they may be. Complaining doesn't get anything accomplished, and worse, it amplifies the problem. If you have something to get off your chest, do it with intention. Tell the person you are venting to, "There's something I want to share so I can gain perspective and move on." Once you're done, tell yourself, *I'm open to seeing this in a different way.*

REVISIT SOMETHING
YOU DON'T LIKE

It's common to make snap judgments that slowly ossify into unwritten rules about what you do and do not like. Yet, it can take the human mind several tries to decide if it likes something new. Consider if there is something you've dismissed in the past that would behoove you to try again. Is there a food you've written off, or a specific task at work? Revisit it. You might surprise yourself.

IMPROVE WHAT YOU CAN

If there's some pesky little thing that's diminishing the quality of your life, it's worth your time to seek out some way of remedying it instead of simply enduring it. Enduring for no good reason is tiring and tiresome. If the light above your garage door is burned out and you almost wipe out on the ice every time you get out of the car, take twenty minutes to get out the ladder and change the bulb this weekend (or call someone who can do it for you). Do what you can to upgrade your experience. It doesn't have to be perfect; it just has to be better.

SMILE MORE

Your facial expressions send signals to your nervous system and can trigger either a stress response or a relaxation response. If you'd like to spend more time in the latter, raise the corners of your lips when you're in conversation as well as when you are engaged in other activities. What about when you're driving? Or checking email? This isn't about appearing friendlier or putting on a facade; it's about raising your barometer for moment-to-moment happiness.

WEAR SOMETHING REMARKABLE

Even if you aren't a fashion plate, wearing a special pin, hat, necklace, or pair of socks can boost your mood and communicate something about your personality to other people. It doesn't have to be fresh from Milan—if you're headed to a picnic where you'll be around new people, wear a favorite sports or band T-shirt instead of a plain white one. This kind of signaling can be an icebreaker in itself. It can also make people feel comfortable saying hello, even if they don't mention what you're wearing. This is especially helpful if you tend to be introverted or shy. Forge a connection by wearing something that will help you stand out while you're busy fitting in.

FIND THE HUMOR

There's a thin line between tragedy and comedy; choosing to see the funny will help pitfalls, big or small, feel less tragic. Try to see the physical comedy in a fall, or the ridiculousness of getting perturbed by a slow barista, or the absurdness of a miscommunication. Laughing about something that's gone "wrong" is a great emotional release, which helps you recover with a clearer head. It also helps you take yourself and your problems a little less seriously, which promotes perspective.

REMEMBER THAT LIFE IS SHORT

The average person lives just twenty-eight thousand days, which may seem like a lot until you consider that ten thousand of those are gone by the time you're in your late twenties. And of course, there are no guarantees. Rather than being morbid, reminding yourself that your time here is finite can help you take a big-picture view, which makes big problems seem smaller and heightens the importance of simple moments.

REMEMBER THAT IT'S ALL A MIRACLE

Consider this: we live on a huge rock that's hurtling through space and we each contain many of the same materials that comprise stars. The very fact that you're alive is a miracle. Remembering these facts can make day-to-day annoyances seem pretty insignificant and inspire you to do things that might otherwise seem impossible.

GO FOR GOOD ENOUGH

There's a point of diminishing returns in always trying to be the very best, as when the fear of failure keeps you from beginning, or when pursuit of perfectionism turns you into a relentless self-critic. This can show up in big ways—the great business or book idea you don't actually take any steps toward creating—and small—assessing your appearance in the mirror multiple times a day, looking for flaws. To break out of this rut, get comfortable with the idea of being good enough. You don't have to be the best ever; you just have to show up, stay open, be real, and do your best. Anything that doesn't go well, you'll learn from. Or laugh about. Or both.

ACT THE FOOL

Asking the "dumb" question, saying the silly thing, and taking the risk of looking goofy on the dance floor are all liberating. After all, once you've made the clown move, what's left to be self-conscious about? Better yet, your example will encourage other people to join you—and anyone who looks down her nose at you isn't someone you want to invest your time in anyway.

MAKE A LIST OF DREAMS

Keeping good ideas floating around in your head is a great way to ensure that they won't happen. Take a tip from writers, who know that the only good ideas that come to life are the ones that get written down. Take out a piece of paper and record everything you'd love to do someday—aim to hit one hundred dreams. You'll have a reminder and motivator to get going on those things that are calling you, and you also won't have the burden of remembering all of them. When you put your dreams into words you begin putting them into action.

BELIEVE THERE IS ENOUGH

Many people grew up with the impression that there simply weren't enough resources to go around, whether it was money, food, time, or affection. As a result, they formed a self-protective belief that maybe they'd never find a job that paid enough, a partner who loved them completely, or the time to do all the things they cared about. But putting stock in the idea of scarcity makes you come from a fearful place, and that's not the kind of place from which anyone makes the best decisions. You don't need there to be thousands of great jobs, suitable partners, or perfect homes. You only need one of each—the one that's right for you.

EMBRACE THE PARADOX OF ACCEPTANCE WITH ANTICIPATION

You can't make peace with what you haven't accepted. And yet, accepting might feel like resignation. Here's a magical thing about this conundrum that you may not have considered: as soon as you accept something—the fact that your kid doesn't like to read (yet), for example, or your current weight—that thing you've been resisting often improves all on its own. Being okay with what is and looking forward to what's to come is a great state to be in, because it crowds out any angst and keeps you focused on the good.

VISUALIZE HAPPINESS

Visualizing is a powerful practice—Olympic great Michael Phelps attributes his consistent high level of performance to a regular habit of visualizing success. Unfortunately, the most common way people visualize is by imagining things going wrong. When you catch yourself thinking about various worst-case scenarios, ask yourself, *Do I really want to rehearse unhappiness*? Use it as a reminder to spend a few seconds envisioning everything working out swimmingly.

SEEK NOVELTY

From an evolutionary perspective, a creature that doesn't evolve is unlikely to thrive or even to survive. As supportive as routine can be, overreliance on the familiar can stagnate your development. A great way to keep your mind open is to expose yourself regularly to new people, ideas, and places. Drive home along a different route, take a class in something you know nothing about, invite someone you don't know very well to coffee—you'll keep your mind sharp and your horizons expanded.

TRY ON "MAYBE"

The word *maybe* gets a bad rap as being noncommittal, but it's a handy tool to keep you from rushing to judgment. For example, is it bad news that your roof is leaking? Well, the leaking is unfortunate, and cleaning up the water may be a pain, but the news might be very fortunate indeed, if you're willing to see it that way. Fixing the leak may uncover a structural issue that would be a much bigger fix if you hadn't found it until next year. Break the habit of labeling things "good" or "bad" to stay more even-keeled and receptive to whatever life brings you.

BE REAL

Every person on this planet has quirks—a funny laugh, a nervous habit, a propensity to do something that could be perceived as odd. Trying to hide those traits takes up a ton of energy and brain space. It also keeps you from bonding with the people who will love you for your idiosyncrasies—and it will make others less likely to let you see their loveable quirks. Let your inner oddball see the light of day: those who are repelled aren't your people anyway.

ACCEPT THE BUMPS

Instead of taking annoyances personally—*Why is this happening to me?*—use them as an occasion to practice effortless effort. Imagine the obstacle is a rock and you are a stream—seek to simply flow around, undeterred, whatever appears to be impeding your progress. Pay inconveniences just as much attention as they require, and keep moving.

CULTIVATE WILLINGNESS

There's probably a habit you want to change. Is it bickering with your partner, eating a bowl of ice cream every night, or watching too much television? Instead of buckling down and trying harder, seek to tap into a sense of willingness to change. You may not be able to access 100 percent willingness at any given time, but often all it takes is 1 percent to start to crack open doors in your mind that lead to happy new changes in your life.

EMBRACE AWKWARDNESS

It's all but impossible to do anything well if you've never done it before. If you want to continue to grow and evolve, you're going to have to be okay with doing things that you don't exactly know how to do (yet), and risk looking a bit silly at first. Make it your aim to be "good enough" and look for the humor. Aim not to take yourself too seriously.

ASK FOR WHAT YOU NEED

There is one person on this earth who knows more than any other person about what you need and want at any given time—you. If you don't speak up and ask for it, it's likely that no one else is going to do it for you. For example, if you need some time alone, articulate that to your spouse: "I am so much happier when I have some alone time at home. Could you find a time to take the kids on an outing without me?" You may think your desires should be obvious, and they are—to you. But they are often not obvious to others. No matter how much you may wish that your partner or colleague could give you what you need unprompted, you are the one responsible for sharing your deepest thoughts and desires, as well as your smallest moment-to-moment needs. Make the ask. When you are your own advocate, you make it easier for people to help you.

MAKE A DATE WITH YOUR MUSE

You don't have to consider yourself an artist to be creative. Everyone has an innate creativity—it's where your best ideas come from. But if you're just waiting for your ingenuity to show up in a bolt out of the blue, you'll likely be waiting a long time. Woo your muse by keeping a consistent appointment with it—a regular time when you get out the journal, fire up the laptop, or get out preferred creative tools. If you keep showing up, so will your good ideas.

KNOW WHEN TO FOLD 'EM

As important as perseverance is, there comes a time in every person's life when the best available move is to surrender—to stop trying to muscle your way through and go for a walk, listen to a favorite piece of music, or do whatever makes you feel like yourself again. When you give your best and then let go of trying to influence the outcome, you create space for grace.

BE COOL WITH THE ITCH

Every itch deserves a scratch—or does it? An itch is not always a physiological necessity; it's often a distraction. Strengthen your capacity for focus by resisting some of those fleeting impulses that you're peppered with all day long—to poke around in the fridge, to check your phone, to watch that next epi-sode. It'll train your mind to stick with what you've chosen to focus on through those inevitable moments of mental discomfort.

SHIELDS UP

Setting an intention for yourself—for the day, a presentation, a conversation—sets a boundary around your thoughts. Before you embark on something, decide how you want to present yourself, or how you want things to go. *I will request an explanation, and I will keep an open mind.* Or, *Today I will take a breath before I respond to anything that annoys me.* Declare an intention to help you stay true to yourself, no matter what happens.

DON'T TREAT GIFTS LIKE BURDENS

Are you using a positive development as a reason to feel bad? Say you got the promotion you've been gunning for: are you now bemoaning the fact that you have to work harder? Every growth opportunity comes with its own set of inconveniences, but these are just the tolls you have to pay to get to the good stuff. Focus on the benefits your efforts are creating for you and those around you, not on the growing pains along the way.

DO SOMETHING NICE FOR THE FUTURE YOU

The best way to take care of the future is to take good care of the present; but thinking about what kind of future you'd like will help you choose what you do in the present. Would the you of tomorrow feel better if you had that second helping of ice cream, or if you didn't? Contemplate what the future version of yourself would want you to do. It's a powerful way to help you make more loving decisions in the present.

MAKE YOUR MOM PROUD

Moms get excited when their kids do things that typically don't get praised once a person reaches adulthood—remembering to say please, following through on a promise, checking in on someone who's sad. Aim to do one thing a day that would make your mom proud to foster these types of everyday kindnesses. (And if you didn't have a great mother, imagine a more loving maternal figure.)

READ INSPIRATIONAL BOOKS

A great book is a teacher, a friend, and a therapist all rolled into one. Read a biography of someone you admire, or a memoir of someone who's faced challenges similar to yours, or a novel in which the heroine triumphs. Reading opens a door in your mind that you could do these things too. It's where imagination meets intellect, and it helps build both.

PART TWO

Connect with Your Feelings

Because emotions seemingly come out of nowhere and can feel overpowering, and because we're not typically given much—or any—education on how to work with them, the thought of getting more in touch with your emotions can seem scary. But it's more like popping a bottle of champagne than opening Pandora's box; there may be a rush at first, but soon it turns into a manageable flow. It's worth the effort to connect with your emotions, because they are messengers—they reveal what you truly think and feel. And without this information, it's impossible to lead with your heart.

As an added bonus, learning to work with your feelings will help you stop acting out of a desire to hide them or ignore them—a natural impulse that typically does not lead to wise choices, whether that's choosing to eat, drink, or bite your lip in an effort to stuff those feelings down; tell a lie to make yourself look better; or jump to getting angry because it's more tolerable then feeling sad or hurt. Managing your emotions feels so much better. And when you feel better, you can do better.

FORGIVE YOUR MISTAKES

It's tempting to ignore your missteps, or worse, to beat yourself up about them. But if you can't forgive yourself for your slipups, you won't be able to forgive others for theirs, which creates a downward spiral of disconnection. Start by taking out a piece of paper and writing "I forgive myself for..." You might be surprised how many things pop into your head, and how cathartic it is to name and release them. Notice how doing it for yourself helps you forgive—and feel closer to—others.

LEARN TO RECOGNIZE YOUR INNER CRITIC

Do you have a mean voice in your head that critiques every little thing, from the shirt you choose to the plans you make? Because it's coming from inside your head, it's hard to be objective about this voice—you may confuse it for truth. But 99.9 percent of the time, it isn't truth at all: that inner critic can be quite a bully. *You'll never be able to pull this off. What are you thinking? You're so stupid.* What kinds of mean things do you think about yourself over and over? Write them down. Seeing them objectively will help you stand up to the negative voice in your head, and you and others will be better off for it.

▢ DRAW YOUR INNER CRITIC

Here's a way to get even more perspective on that mean inner voice: draw a picture of it, even if you "can't" draw. Does it wear glasses? Have a mustache? How old is it? Drawing the critic helps you see that this voice is not you, and also helps you laugh at it a bit, which can deflate the stress that voice creates.

▢ LEARN THE SECRET OF LETTING GO

If there's a situation that's weighing you down, how do you let it go? Imagine whatever it is encapsulated inside a balloon, and that you're holding the string in your hand. Then see yourself releasing that string and watching the balloon float off into the ether. If it doesn't let go easily, take an imaginary pair of scissors to it. When you start thinking about it again, which you likely will, remind yourself, *I've chosen to move on.*

☐ IDENTIFY YOUR TRIGGERS

When something happens that makes you really upset—either the kind of upset that doesn't fade quickly or the kind that's out of proportion to the size of the offense—take a moment to ask yourself why it's causing such a reaction. What fear, hurt, or resentment is getting triggered? When you can recognize which button is getting pushed, it will help you respond more thoughtfully to the current situation and may point toward an old wound that deserves some of your attention.

☐ PUT YOUR TRIGGERS TO GOOD USE

Once you have more awareness of your emotional triggers, you can use them to your advantage. When they get activated, use it as a reminder to do something nice for yourself, whether that's taking a few deep breaths, going to a favorite place, or booking a session with your therapist. This way you'll be able to lessen your reactions over time.

MANAGE YOUR EMOTIONS BY FOCUSING ON YOUR VALUES

Use your values to help you navigate tricky emotions and sticky situations. If you're feeling anxious about telling a friend something uncomfortable (her ex is dating someone new, say), think about which of your values is being challenged. If it's kindness, ask yourself if it is kinder for her to hear this information from a friend or for her to stay unaware. If it's the former, you can mitigate some of your anxiety by knowing that you're acting on a value you hold dear.

RELINQUISH GUILT

Guilt has a limited purpose—it can point out how you didn't live up to a value. But at some point, it becomes a tool of self-punishment. It's also self-perpetuating: guilt leads to defensiveness, which leads to lashing out, which probably creates another thing to feel guilty about. The insidious thing about guilt is that it can become habitual. Forgive yourself and experience how good it feels to not carry around the perpetual pit in your stomach. In your mind or in your journal, tell yourself, *I did the best I could at the time; next time I will do better.* And then keep your word.

SEEK SOLITUDE

Of course we need to connect with others—humans are pack animals. But we also need the flip side of the coin. Spending time alone helps you reconnect to your own thoughts. This becomes more important the more others depend on you. Think about how much time you spend on your own versus how often you're in the company of others, and get creative about how to give yourself enough alone time to hear what you really think, feel, and want. Spend time alone when you can, and recharge.

INVITE REFLECTION

Take your solitude up a notch by spending some of that time with a journal, a pen, and an open mind. You can simply put your pen on the paper and challenge yourself to write nonstop for ten minutes. Even if all you write is "I don't know what to say," it will help declutter your mind. Once you get going, direct your thoughts by asking yourself, *What do I need in this particular moment?* or *Where do I want to go from here?* When you make room for it, the reflective part of your mind will guide you toward learning and growth.

PRAY

It doesn't matter who or what you pray to, but sharing your thoughts with a higher power has been shown again and again to be beneficial for your physical and emotional health. Atheists confirm it: many report feeling mentally and emotionally lighter after sharing their thoughts with a cloud, the moon, even a ceiling fan. Saying whatever kind of prayer feels right to you, whenever it occurs to you, will help you feel more supported and unburdened. Don't know what to say? Simply saying "thank you" is a nice way to nurture a spiritual connection.

MEDITATE

Meditation does three crucial things: it promotes relaxation, trains you to start again when you get off track, and teaches you to not chase every distracting thought that pops into your head. To meditate, don't overthink it—set a timer for five to fifteen minutes and simply sit and focus on the sound of your breathing. When your mind wanders, say the word *thinking* in your mind and go back to the breath. Repeat until the timer goes off. Meditate again tomorrow.

◻ DROP YOUR SKEPTICISM

We all need a bit of skepticism—you don't want to buy a lemon simply because you didn't think to look under the hood. But making sure you never get snookered can become a habit that hardens your heart and mind, which in turn makes you less trustworthy to others. To strike a balance, seek to understand instead of reject, and to gather information rather than expose flaws.

◻ HEAR YOUR BROKEN RECORD

The things you tell yourself over and over shape your worldview. So, what do you say again and again? If you aren't sure, ask your partner and some trusted friends what they hear you say repeatedly. Things like: "It must be nice to have that much money." "Life's a bitch." "We're so broke." What are some new, more positive phrases you can replace them with?

FIND A KINDER INNER VOICE

Once you get a handle on what your unique inner voice sounds like, you can take steps to upgrade it (after all, you can't change a habit you don't know you have). How would Glinda the Good Witch talk to you? Or your dog? Or your best friend? Choose whose guidance you want to internalize and give yourself an alternative to the same old meanie. Change your inner voice and it won't be long before you and others notice new warmth in your outer voice too.

DEVELOP DISCERNMENT

To discern means to perceive and to distinguish—it's a lot subtler than judging and reacting. And it's a skill that can be honed. Next time you're faced with a choice, aim to discern the step that makes the most sense for you. Coming from this perspective implies that choice already exists and you don't have to do the work of creating it. Practice discerning rather than deciding, and help yourself choose a little more courageously.

◼ TRUST YOUR GUT

Your intuition is the wise part of yourself that senses what's in your best interest and what's not. The problem is, intuition speaks quietly, and sometimes cryptically—kind of like Yoda—so it's easy to ignore or dismiss. Strengthen your relationship with your inner Yoda by letting it make at least one decision a day, such as what to work on next or who to reach out to. Just as in any other relationship, the more you listen to your intuition, the more you understand what it's trying to say.

◼ BE YOUR OWN BEST FRIEND

Buddhists describe the aim of meditation as "making friends with yourself." That can be a pretty novel concept if you typically think of yourself as someone or something to critique. If you were your own best friend, how would you treat yourself differently? What shortcomings would you accept? What accomplishments would you be proud of? Another benefit of this activity is that you'll likely find yourself inspired to be a better friend to others.

☐ KNOW HOW YOU RECHARGE BEST

If you're wondering why you always feel worn out, you may not be giving yourself the right conditions you need to rejuvenate. Introverts require solitude, while extroverts need to be around other people. If you don't know much about your personality type, take an online Myers-Briggs personality test—you'll be surprised how much it can help you understand the conditions you need to feel your best.

☐ AIM TO ACCEPT

You may wish your spouse were more organized or your child were more successful, but wanting them to be different than they are only weighs you down. Until you drop your resistance and accept them as they are you won't be able to find understanding or peace—and they won't find it with you. The more you remind your spouse to put his wallet in the same spot every night, the more he'll be inspired to comment on the habits of yours that drive him crazy (how it takes you so long to answer a text, say). When you accept that he's a messy guy, he's more likely to find his way to a new habit, because he won't feel compelled to rebel against you. The magical thing about acceptance is that once you can access it, the thing you were resisting often changes all on its own—the dynamic shifts and new possibilities open up.

INVESTIGATE YOUR DISDAIN

The behaviors that bug you typically mean one of two things. One possibility: you recognize that trait in yourself but don't want to accept it, so you demonize someone for it rather than acknowledge it in yourself. Another: it's something that you never let yourself do and it drives you crazy that other people think it's okay. Investigate why something irritates and you'll shine a light on a corner of your internal attic that could use a little decluttering.

MAKE PEACE WITH GRIEF

Grief comes in waves that may feel like tsunamis, but it's in your best interest to let it wash over you. Unexpressed grief doesn't go away—it goes underground and then seeps out in other ways, be it anger, despair, or numbness. And while it requires reflective time too, the grieving process wants us to reach out to others for support. Find the resources you need to steady yourself, whether that's a mental health professional, a book, a support group, or a trusted friend. There's a gift waiting for you on the other side if you allow it.

STOP WAITING TO BE DONE

It's common to think *I'm going to get everything on my to-do list done and then I'm going to relax.* But if you're waiting for your plate to be completely empty before you feel content, you're going to be waiting a long time. Too long. (Perhaps forever.) Also, the busier you are, the more you need relaxation. Contentment is an inside job, so stop waiting for external circumstances to create it for you.

CHOOSE LOVE

If you have a big decision to make, you can make pro and con lists from now until next Christmas, but you'll only be using one part of your intelligence, and not the most insightful part. To access your inner wisdom, frame your decision in terms of *What would create the highest good for me and everyone else affected by this decision*? It will help you get out of the rational mind, which is probably mostly focused on keeping you protected—and preventing change.

☐ DEAL WITH YOUR "STUFF"

Maybe there's something in your past that left a scar, a wound that never healed completely. You may think that it happened so long ago that it's water under the bridge, but healing isn't one-and-done. It's a process. Now that you've matured and put some distance between yourself and the original event, you also have more perspective. There's always more insight and closure available, and you deserve to have the peace that those two things can bring. Whether you work with a therapist or other counselor or start opening up to a trusted friend or your journal, grant yourself the permission to devote some energy to coming to terms with old hurts. It will not only help you improve your relationship with yourself, but it will also help you connect more fully with others, because you'll be less guarded.

☐ COME BACK TO THE PRESENT

The mind loves to time travel, dreading what hasn't happened yet, or replaying what's already occurred. This leaves you in a pickle, because the present moment is where your life is happening! To come back to now, feel your feet on the ground, your butt on the seat, or the sun on your cheek. You may need to "come back" several times a day. It's not the fact that you wander off that matters; it's making sure you remember to come back home.

MAKE PEACE WITH THE THINGS THAT IRRITATE YOU

What secretly—or not so secretly—bugs you? Is it the way your partner chews? Hearing your kids say your name twelve times in two minutes? People who don't pick up their dog's poop? Think about things you regularly encounter that give you a flicker of irritation and choose to use them as reminders to take a breath. You'll feel better in the moment, and you'll respond more thoughtfully.

SEEK POISE DURING DELAYS

Flights don't leave on time, traffic happens, projects hit a snag, things take longer than you think they should. Thinking you should be further along increases your angst when the reality is: timing is beyond your control. Impatience doesn't make things happen more quickly; it just makes you feel worse. To practice maintaining poise, tell yourself, *I trust that things are happening at the perfect time.*

LOOK UNDER THE ROCK
OF YOUR ANGER

When something sets you off, resist the urge toward righteous indignation and look deeper. Anger is generally caused by emotions that require a little more vulnerability to process, such as hurt or fear. You may not want to "go there" in the moment, but once you've cooled off, let yourself see what feelings are hiding under the anger. When a coworker takes credit for your idea, for example, you may get good (and rightly) ticked off, but once your anger has subsided a bit, you may see that it wasn't just the act itself that upset you—it was the betrayal of trust by your colleague and perhaps frustration at yourself for not having put forth the idea to your boss sooner. Once you know what's at the root, you'll be able to decide on a next step that brings peace instead of more strife (in this instance, instead of bad-mouthing your colleague, you can be more discerning about who you trust at work and start putting your own ideas forward).

RECOGNIZE WHEN IT'S YOU
YOU'RE MAD AT

Anger can be a sneaky way to avoid taking responsibility. Next time you're miffed, ask, are you mad at the slow driver in front of you or are you angry with yourself because you left ten minutes too late—again? If you don't like what you're getting, owning your role can save everyone a lot of agita.

BE THANKFUL FOR THE LESSON

Experience is an inefficient way to learn, perhaps—if only you could learn everything you need before you made any mistakes! But experience is often the only thing that can teach you the exact lesson you need to learn. Sometimes, the only way to learn is to learn the hard way—whether that's having your heart broken by the person who seemed so attentive but who ended up being a master manipulator, or learning the lesson of never leaving the house without a diaper after being caught unprepared on your first trip to the grocery store with baby. Accepting the lesson with as much gratitude as you can muster will make learning by experience feel much less painful. Be glad you took the hard route, and learn from it.

FIND YOUR MENTAL HAPPY PLACE

Just like the brain can't tell the difference between an imaginary threat and a real one (the way your heart races while watching a scary movie), it also struggles with the difference between a pretend vacation and the real thing. Spend a few moments each day thinking about what it feels like to be in one of your favorite spots on earth. It'll help reset your resting mood to one of relaxation.

APPRECIATE MORE

Appreciation is one degree of separation away from gratitude. Appreciation is a fabulous attitude to cultivate, because in order to appreciate something you have to stop and take it in, which means you're in the present moment and not off somewhere in your head. Appreciation directs your attention toward what's going right, and when you focus on something it grows (or, you could say, what you appreciate appreciates—as in, it increases in value).

REHEARSE HAPPINESS

How often do you actually daydream about how good it will feel when all the things you are working on pan out? It's much more common to imagine various worst-case scenarios, because the brain is wired to look for potential problems. Visualizing a happy ending can act like a tractor beam, inspiring you to take the steps that will lead you to that point. So instead of worrying about messing up at the big meeting, spend a moment thinking about returning to your desk with a spring in your step after delivering a great presentation—it will train your brain to do what it takes to recreate that feeling.

RISK A BIGGER DREAM

As you grow into a better version of yourself, it's likely that your horizons will expand and you'll be able to see new opportunities that you hadn't previously considered. Perhaps a promotion at work opens the door to speaking opportunities, for example, or learning to become a better communicator attracts new, more satisfying relationships. Whatever possibility presents itself, lean into it. Going after a bigger goal will make you stronger, and help you realize that many of the things you thought were impossible are actually within your reach. Dare to dream a bigger dream for yourself.

FIND A HEALTHY OUTLET FOR YOUR ANGER

Anger's a perfectly human emotion and not something you have to stuff down. At the same time, it's not okay to go flying off the handle at other people simply because you're ticked off. Find nonharmful ways to release anger—vigorous cleaning, long runs, deep breaths, or primal screams in the car are all good options (and there are many more—keep experimenting). The only guiding principle here is to find the one that works for you, without harming those around you.

JOURNAL

Writing your thoughts on a piece of paper can be incredibly freeing. Not only do you not have to carry them around in your head anymore, but you also get the chance to read back what you wrote, which can be very enlightening. There is no "right" way to do it—just set your pen on the paper and see what comes out. There's nothing you can't say here, so use your journal as an opportunity to get your crazy out!

NAME YOUR FEELINGS

To work with your feelings instead of simply being taken for a ride by them, aim to identify exactly what emotion you're experiencing. In order to name it, you have to allow yourself to feel it. So, instead of trying to talk yourself out of that initial rush of indignation when you feel a friend has slighted you, pause long enough to allow yourself to experience the physical sensations of your upset—the flush in your cheeks, the tightening in your belly. Say out loud, "I am so angry right now I feel like flames might shoot out the top of my head!" It doesn't mean you act on your anger; it simply means you experience it. Ironically, the more you can feel that angry feeling, the faster it will move on, as suppressed feelings don't go away—they just go into hiding. When you recognize what you're feeling and call it what it is, you'll help yourself move through it.

TEACH KIDS TO RECOGNIZE THEIR OWN EMOTIONS

Help increase your kids' emotional intelligence by encouraging them to identify their feelings and discuss them with you. Ask them to draw faces that reflect different emotional states or have them act out various feelings—and let them know that whatever they feel is okay. While you can't manage your children's emotions, making their feelings less mysterious will help them navigate some of the tumult of growing up.

IDENTIFY HOW YOUR FEELINGS FEEL

Emotions don't just happen in your mind—they have a physical component to them. For example, when you're sad, you cry. In the name of further demystifying feelings, start to assess where you are feeling your feelings when you experience them. Is there a tightness in your throat? A fluttery feeling in your stomach? A burning in your chest? Again, this will help you feel your feelings, which is the best way to help them move along.

STOP SQUIRRELING AWAY
THE GOOD STUFF

Sure, it's nice to have fancy things, but why keep them tucked away until a special occasion? Wear that pretty nightgown. Eat off the good plates. Use your artisanal soap. In other words, don't save pleasure for another day. This is especially true with heirloom items, such as Grandma's china or the family silverware. Let your children, your friends, and everyone in your life have fun with them—it's what your forebearers did! Enjoy the finer things in your life now to raise your overall happiness quotient.

CHOOSE THE PEOPLE YOU
CONFIDE IN WISELY

Sharing your feelings with someone else can be such a powerful experience—it has the potential to make you feel heard and validated, which is a beautiful thing. What's not so great is sharing your feelings with someone who tells you you're overreacting, or immediately tells you what you should do, or judges you. You don't have to share your feelings with everyone— choose who you reveal yourself to with care.

ACCEPT COMPLIMENTS

When someone tells you you've done a good job, resist the temptation to brush it off (*Oh, it was nothing*) or point out something you didn't do well (*Too bad I forgot the most important part!*). Just let it in. It's not vain or attention-seeking. It's someone attempting to pay you a kindness, and rejecting it just keeps you and the other person from feeling good.

ACCEPT CRITICISM

Being critiqued can be scary, but we all need help seeing our blind spots. If you can be open to asking for and taking in feedback—the negative as well as the positive— you'll be better equipped to do better next time. When you interview for a job you wanted but didn't get, for example, take a deep breath, swallow hard, and say to the interviewer, "I'm very interested in improving my interviewing skills. Could you offer any insight as to how I could present myself better?" If you can set the stage for a helpful dialogue and stay open enough to hear and objectively assess what the other person has to say, you're likely to glean a piece of information that can make all the difference. If the criticism you receive is mean-spirited, aim to accept that the other person has his own opinion without taking it on as fact. It's feedback. Remember that you want to be heard when someone else's actions affect you negatively, and so do those around you.

☐ RESIST THE URGE FOR VENGEANCE

It's so tempting to want to *crush* someone who has hurt you, but when you seek vengeance, you only perpetuate the cycle of harm. You may not be able to leap to forgiveness, and sometimes maybe you shouldn't. But if you can at least resist the urge to strike back when you've been struck, you'll give yourself an opportunity to reflect and then respond. This tends to pave a smoother path than simply reacting, which often just creates more ripples.

☐ LET GO OF BLAME

When things go wrong, your inner critic will seek to deflect any potential criticism by blaming someone else— *It wasn't me, it was her*! Resist the urge to shift all responsibility onto another party—as an adult, there are very few experiences that you don't play some role in. Admitting how you contributed to a failure may be painful— because you have to admit how you fell short—but it will help you identify what you can do differently, and better, next time.

UPGRADE YOUR TRIBE

Germs aren't the only things that are contagious—research has shown that smoking, obesity, and depression tend to run in social circles. Meaning the people you hang out with have a lot to do with how happy and healthy you are. If your current friends aren't interested in also being better people, or get threatened by your efforts to become one, find some new friends who are supportive. Perhaps seeing you make changes—even from afar—will inspire your old friends to make their own changes for the better.

ASK FOR HELP WHEN YOU NEED IT

You don't get extra points for doing something completely on your own. Asking for help makes you take stock of what you need and gives someone else the chance to do something for you, which gives them an opportunity to feel good. It also makes you feel supported and connected, and that's when you can be your best.

PART THREE

Be Healthy

It's hard to be a better person if you're feeling tired, stressed, or sick. Taking better care of yourself gives you more energy for the important stuff *and* the fun stuff. Feeling great physically also translates to feeling great mentally. When your body is humming, your thinking gets clearer, which helps you continue to make the choices that lead to being a better person.

Thankfully, getting healthier doesn't mean you have to completely overhaul your diet or your life. This chapter contains suggestions for simple lifestyle changes you can make to live a healthier life, that are easy to implement yet yield big results. Each one will put more fuel in your tank to keep you going and help you feel great along the way. If you ever feel your momentum start to stall, return to this chapter and choose another one or two things you can do to support your body, so it can support you and your efforts.

CHANGE YOUR DEFAULT REACTION TO STRESS

You may not realize it, but you have a go-to reaction to stress. You may jump to anger, or dive into self-criticism, or feel overwhelmed. Maybe you reach for cookies or start skimping on sleep. What does your stress pattern look like? Write it down, then make a list of things you could do instead of those old standbys—taking a walk, making a cup of tea, belting out a song on the car ride home, or getting in a warm bath before bed are all helpful options. Even if you try one new thing before you start rummaging in the snack drawer, you'll have interrupted your knee-jerk response. Responding to life with intention, rather than by reaction, is almost always a better approach.

REMIND YOURSELF OF PAST TRIUMPHS

You can't escape stress, but you can learn to not let it escalate into a full-blown panic attack. Make a list of times when you handled a stressful situation well—when you organized a complicated move, for example, or met a big deadline at work—and look at it whenever you're feeling strapped. It will help remind you that yes, you do have what it takes, and that this too shall pass.

TAKE A TIME-OUT

It may feel like you've got to move at top speed to stay ahead of your to-do list, but slowing down for even a moment can help you get more done with less stress. Challenge yourself periodically throughout the day to do nothing for a few moments—after you sit at your desk but before you turn on the computer, or while you wait for the coffee to brew. Practicing a good pace at these low-stakes times will help you remember to do the same when something seemingly urgent is happening, and will make you more effective when acting under stress.

IDENTIFY YOUR BAD HABITS

Do you intend to drink only one glass of wine, but always end up having two? Do you forget to eat lunch and then have a snack attack every afternoon? Let yourself see your bad habits and their consequences. Write them down so you can be objective. If you have trouble recognizing your bad habits, ask a trustworthy friend or family member to help you identify them. You obviously can't change a habit if you aren't aware of it. The point here isn't to beat yourself up, but to raise your awareness of your shortcomings. Everyone has bad habits, but not everyone recognizes them.

☐ RECOGNIZE WHEN YOUR BAD HABITS
ARE LEADING THE WAY

Once you know your bad habits, spend some time thinking about what triggers them. Are you reaching for wine because you've got no other outlet for your stress? Are you raiding the vending machine because you were too busy to eat lunch? It's not the actions themselves that need addressing, it's the conditions that create them. If you address those, changing the bad habit becomes a lot more manageable.

☐ USE YOUR BREATH TO STAY GROUNDED
DURING TENSE MOMENTS

When something stressful happens, your breath can be the anchor that keeps you from being swept away in a tide of anxiety. Aiming your breath into your belly for three breaths, for example, shifts focus away from your swirling thoughts. It also engages your diaphragm, which tells your body that it's okay to call off the stress response. Try this: inhale for four, hold for two, and exhale for six—the extended out-breath will calm your nervous system. When stress mounts, breathe your way through.

PRIORITIZE SELF-CARE

It's all too easy to put yourself last on your list of things to take care of. Self-care isn't limited to getting a massage—it means staying in touch with your needs and taking steps to meet them. It includes eating when you're hungry, sleeping when you're tired, and talking it out when you're upset. After all, you can't give from an empty cup. You deserve as much of your attention as do all your various responsibilities. Consider this paragraph to be all the permission you need to tend to yourself accordingly.

BUILD RESILIENCE THROUGH CONSCIOUS RELAXATION

In order to be able to perform well, you also have to be able to relax well—it helps you come back to balance and gives you more reserves to draw on when it's go-time. That doesn't mean charging through your binge-watch list, however: entertainment, while engrossing, is not relaxing. Stretch, meditate, spend time in nature, do yoga, journal—all of these help you get into the physiological state of relaxation.

MOVE MORE

Spending too much time in one position is stressful to the body—which was designed for movement—and can lead to all sorts of physical woes, including aches and even disease. You don't have to become a gym rat. You just have to get moving—walk more places, hit the playground with your kids instead of sitting on the bench, go dancing for date night. You'll lubricate your joints, strengthen your muscles, breathe better, improve digestion, and get better sleep. This holds true at work as well, even if you are required to sit at your desk throughout the day. Take a ten-minute walk away from your desk, and without shame. Invite your coworkers along!

TAKE UP A MIND-BODY PRACTICE

A mind-body practice is any activity that gets your mind and body on the same page—meditation, tai chi, yoga, kung fu, and jujitsu are just some examples. While there are different forms, they all help you become more at home in your body and more disciplined in your thinking—two key components for being a better person. There is no right one, only the one that you enjoy so much that you'll stick to it.

LET YOUR BODY LEAD THE WAY

Whether you call it a knowing in your bones or a gut feeling, your body is where your wisdom lives. If you have a habit of ignoring your body, it's going to be harder to hear that wise voice. Cultivate that mind-body relationship by heeding your body's cues—eat when you're hungry, drink when you're thirsty, go to the bathroom when you have to go to the bathroom, and go to bed when you're tired. Better to wait on that next episode than to ignore your intuition. When you act as the master of your own body, you also set a fantastic example for children and adults alike.

GET POSTURE-SAVVY

If you're spending the majority of your waking hours with poor posture, you're causing excessive wear and tear on your joints and impeding your breathing and digestion (for starters). Pilates, yoga, the Alexander Technique, and the Feldenkrais Method all teach better posture. If you have chronic physical tension, consider investing in some lessons for one or more of these techniques. Even a simple postural adjustment such as sliding your chin back until your ears are aligned with your shoulders makes a big difference in your neck and shoulder tension—and yes, in your appearance too. When you exhibit better posture, people will notice. Nothing wrong with that!

ASSESS YOUR VICES

Being a better person doesn't mean you have to be vir-tuous 100 percent of the time. The question is, do your vices cause more pain than pleasure? Does your nightly wine interfere with your sleep and make you feel guilty? Is that late-night bowl of ice cream preventing you from feeling good about the way you look? A vice can be an indulgent treat or it can be a sneaky way of sabotaging yourself. Know which one is which. If you still can't tell, ask someone (very) close to you—chances are if you have a vice that's holding you back, your nearest and dearest know just what it is.

AVOID EXCESS

Big highs—from a chocolate binge, too many drinks, even a shopping spree—are followed by lows of equal intensity (when the stomachache, hangover, or credit card bill arrives). Practice more sensible servings of the indulgences you crave. How about one new skirt instead of three? A bite and not the bar, a glass instead of the whole bottle. There's another rush waiting behind the relief you'll feel in the morning. When it comes to treats, sometimes a little goes further than a lot.

☐ TAKE A SABBATH

This is among the most ancient and enduring pieces of wisdom in this book: at least once a month spend a day not doing things—no working, no errands, no chores. Just be, either by yourself or with people you love. Whether or not you conceive of this "day of rest" as a commandment, it's a helpful and important reminder—to yourself, to your coworkers, and to your loved ones—that you are more than a productivity engine. As are they. When you take an intentional break from the drive to get things done, you'll come back to your regular life seeing things differently, and you'll be energized to do them differently too.

☐ START YOUR DAY RIGHT

How you start anything sets the tone for everything that comes after. Apply this basic truth to your daily life by developing a healthy routine for your mornings. (Meaning, don't roll over and immediately check your email on your phone.) It doesn't have to be elaborate; do a couple of stretches, jot down five things you're grateful for, or visualize the day. Start the day with a clear head and you'll make better decisions all day.

INTERACT WITH NATURE

Whether or not you feel like it, you are a part of the natural world. Spending nearly all your time inside is like depriving yourself of a vital nutrient. Boosting your contact with the natural world doesn't have to be strenuous. Open your bedroom windows, have your coffee outside, hang a birdfeeder on your kitchen window, or drag your coworkers out to eat lunch in the park. Drive home with the windows down! The fresh air and the sunshine will do wonders for your well-being.

EAT YOUR FRUITS AND VEGETABLES

Fresh produce is some of the healthiest and tastiest food you can consume. Make eating fruits and vege-tables your first priority—they'll fill you up and give you a mega-dose of nutrients, crowding out room in your stomach for less nutritious foods. Juices, sal-sas, soups, and stews are all great ways to eat your veggies without the risk of burning out on salads. If you're raising young kids, you'll be amazed how their tastes follow your own when it comes to healthy snacks. You'll be more regular, you'll be more nour-ished, and your body will thank you for it.

MASTER ONE HEALTHY RECIPE EACH WEEK FOR THREE MONTHS

Revamping your diet can be a daunting challenge—so daunting that you don't actually get around to doing it. Rather than making sweeping changes, aim to try out one healthy recipe each week. Since you really only need about a dozen recipes to be able to cook most of your meals and not get bored by lack of variety, you'll have a whole new repertoire of healthy homemade meals in just one season.

GET DOWN ON THE GROUND

Give your couch a rest and sit on the floor more. (You can sit on a cushion or two if it's more comfortable.) While you're down there, it'll be easy to do a few stretches that help you purge stress and stay resilient. Being able to get up and down from the floor is a major marker of health as you age; whether it's tomorrow or someday, aim to be the grandparent who happily gets down on the floor with the kids.

TAKE STOCK OF YOUR SELF-CARE SUPPLIES

Taking better care of yourself helps you perform better. This will help: take stock of your supplies and see what you need to be able to tend to minor ailments as they arise—cold remedies, immune-boosting supplements, Epsom salts for extra-relaxing baths, and a foam roller to roll away aches will all help you stay in your sweet spot.

BEDITATE

As powerful as a mind-body practice is, it doesn't have to be perfect in order to count. You can do yoga in the kitchen while you wait for the coffee to brew, or do ten minutes of tai chi in your bedroom before a busy day, or meditate before you even get out of bed. Sure, longer sessions are important, but when you don't have time for them, the little things you can do absolutely count, and they keep your momentum going.

RETHINK INSOMNIA

There are many physiological reasons for insomnia, but sometimes the root is more psychological or even spiritual in nature. If you can't sleep, is there something happening in your life that perhaps you're not slowing down enough to notice during your waking hours? Is there an idea that needs the quiet of night to get through? Pay attention to that middle-of-the-night message and you'll be more likely to get some sleep.

DEVELOP A BEDTIME ROUTINE

We teach our kids how to get ready for bedtime, but we rarely do the same for ourselves. Help yourself shift gears from wakefulness to sleep with a simple routine that extends just a bit beyond brushing your teeth and changing into jammies: stretch, journal, read something inspirational, give yourself a foot rub. Don't overthink it—the most important part is that it's simple enough to do regularly.

KNOW YOUR MOTIVATION

There's so much advice on how to get healthier and much of it can feel like one big "should." To keep your health-promoting adventures compelling, write down all the reasons why you want to be healthier and put it somewhere you'll see it all the time—on the refrigerator, in your planner, or tucked in your gym bag. Whether it's looking great in your jeans, beating cancer, or seeing your grandchild get married, reviewing your motivations will help you keep going.

GET LIGHT SAVVY

Light doesn't just help you see; it also plays a role in setting your internal clock. Light toward the blue end of the spectrum—such as daylight, LEDs, and the light emitted from electronic devices—is stimulating, while light on the red end of the spectrum—sunsets, candle flames, and firelight—is soothing. Bring bright light into your morning by throwing open the curtains or going outside to soak up some early sunshine; turn off overhead lights, dim the light on your computer screen, and light some candles at night. Either or both tactics will help regulate your sleep, your energy, and your mood.

GO OUTSIDE EVEN WHEN YOU DON'T LIKE THE WEATHER

The outdoors beckon most of us when the sun is shining and the temperature's perfect. But all types of weather offer benefits—rain is refreshing, wind is stimulating, heat is purifying, and cold builds resilience. Going outside when conditions aren't ideal will also help you break the habit of waiting for "the perfect time" in other parts of your life, and give you more chances for great moments with loved ones.

☐ GO OUTSIDE AT NIGHT

Going outside at night exposes you to starlight, moon-light, and darkness—simple things we take for granted in our age of electricity. Also, it's pretty much impossible to see the stars if you're always indoors after dark, and a starlit sky is one of the most beautiful, thought-provoking vistas there is. A nighttime walk is also a great way to break the habit of watching a screen until it's time to pass out. If you have young children it's a must, and if you don't have them do it anyway: gaze up at the night sky.

☐ MAKE MORE OF YOUR OWN FOOD

The best way to upgrade your nutrition is to prepare more of your own food, because you get to hand-select the ingredients and control their quality. Beyond that, cooking is creative, it's tactile, it's movement, and you get to eat the results of it! If you can consider making your own food as a way to show yourself and the people you're feeding some TLC, it will help you see it as less of a chore.

DRINK MORE WATER

Water lubricates your joints, removes toxins and waste from the body, curbs hunger, and promotes digestion. When you cultivate a habit of drinking water regularly, you crowd out higher-calorie beverages and make it much easier to maintain a healthy weight or even lose weight. Pausing to drink a glass of water can even clear your head (because dehydration causes foggy thinking). Best of all, it's mostly free. Drink more water.

UPGRADE YOUR BEVERAGES

Your beverage choices play a huge role in your health, so choose them wisely. If you drink soda, trying switching to kombucha (a fizzy probiotic drink). If you drink sweetened coffee drinks, experiment with stevia (which doesn't spike your blood sugar levels) instead of sugar. If you drink black tea, try green tea (for its antioxidants) or herbal teas (for a variety of health benefits, depending on what you choose). One subtle upgrade can add up to big-time benefits.

☐ COOK A LITTLE EXTRA

When you cook, make enough to have leftovers. Make a big pot of soup on Sunday and have the leftovers for lunch during the week. Roast extra potatoes and sauté a whole bag of spinach, then use those leftovers to make a frittata for dinner in minutes the next night. This way, you only need to really cook a couple of times a week yet still have homemade food every night.

☐ WORK OUT YOUR KINKS

Massages are a useful tool for keeping your body pain-free, but you don't have to wait for an appointment to get relief. Tennis balls make great self-massagers—roll your bare feet over them, or place them under your back while you lie on the floor. Stretching on your own is also a great way to work out the kinks and keep yourself supple. Reach your arms up over your head while you wait for your toast to toast, sit on the floor with your legs in a wide straddle during a commercial to stretch your hips and legs. Remember, you don't have to wait for someone else to make your body feel better.

DO MORE SQUATS

Squats are one of the most efficient whole-body movements to build and maintain strength—they help you build bone strength and make you better equipped for things like running, walking, and jumping. Doing three sets of ten squats, even with no extra weight, is a great five-minute workout that will keep paying dividends as you get older, and will perhaps even make it so that you won't need one of those chairs with a motorized lift in your golden years.

CHALLENGE YOUR BALANCE

You might not give balance much thought until you lose your footing, but developing your ability to stay upright builds all kinds of good things, including core strength, body awareness, and mental focus. To strengthen your balance, stand on one foot while you brush your teeth, try tree pose before bed, or buy a wobble board—you'll love the greater poise you get from learning to withstand balance challenges.

DO EXERCISE THAT DOESN'T FEEL LIKE "WORKING OUT"

Your doctor would love you to be in better shape, but that doesn't necessarily mean you've got to join a gym. There are all kinds of movements that get your heart rate up and help you break a sweat. Gardening, roller-skating, hiking, dancing, etc.—it all counts, and whatever you enjoy, you'll do more of, which is ultimately the most important feature of a fitness regimen.

EAT FEWER LOW-QUALITY CALORIES

As important as it is to think about eating the foods you need more of—primarily fruits and vegetables—you also want to eat less of the stuff that's not great for you. Wean yourself off processed foods by considering what each meal offers your body in terms of fuel or energy. Processed food packages often make a lot of health claims, but you need to read the ingredients and nutritional label for an objective look at a food's inherent value.

☐ FIND OTHER WAYS TO CELEBRATE

Celebrations are a major saboteur of healthy eating. Birthday cake, holiday cookies, Valentine's Day chocolates, Halloween candy—what's supposed to be special occasions can turn into nothing more than day after day of unhealthy eating. Break the chain by developing new celebration traditions that don't revolve around decadent food or drinks. Go someplace special, ask everyone to write a haiku, light sparklers—you'll create memories and you won't go to bed regretting how much you ate.

☐ STRENGTHEN YOUR GRIP

Grip strength is an important predictor of longevity and indicator of cardiovascular health, and according to research, millennials have 10 percent less of it than any previous generation—perhaps those swipe screens and automatic can openers are having unintended consequences. To improve your grip strength, carry more, hang from things (a tree branch or a jungle gym or chin-up bar), and give firmer handshakes. And use the manual can opener!

■ LIFT WEIGHTS

Strength training is like investing for retirement—the effort you spend now will pay big dividends in the decades to come, as lifting weights strengthens your bones, heart, and muscles. And it is so gratifying to see the number of pounds or reps you can do grow. It's also incredibly useful, whether you want to carry your groceries, shovel snow, lift your suitcase, or pick up your kids (or grandkids). No matter how old you are, it's not too late to start.

■ COOK WITH MORE SPICES AND HERBS

Add more oomph—both in flavor and nutrition— to your home-cooked meals by using more spices (which are the seeds of plants) and herbs (the leaves or stems). Each one has its own unique health benefit. Garlic is antiviral and antibacterial, ginger and fennel promote digestion, turmeric is anti-inflammatory, and cinnamon regulates blood sugar, for example. Cooking with these culinary accessories can turn something that tastes okay into something delicious. Be willing to experiment and you'll be rewarded in multiple ways.

☐ CHANGE UP HOW YOU SIT

Whether in the car, at work, or in leisure hours, people are sitting more than ever, and research has consistently found that the more people sit, the worse their health. That doesn't necessarily mean you have to stand the majority of the day, however. You merely need to change the position of your body more frequently, because the real peril of sitting in a chair is that your body stays in the same shape for hours on end, which negatively impacts your joints, muscles, circulation, digestion, and immunity. So, yes, stand and walk more when it makes sense (don't automatically grab a seat on the subway, stand up for conference calls, and walk to the post office instead of driving). But also, when you do sit, change your position and even your location for greater ranges and variety of motion: sit cross-legged in your plane seat, have a picnic dinner on the living room rug, plop down on the floor instead of the couch to watch your favorite show. Your body will thank you, your mind will enjoy the novelty, and you just may end up living longer (and certainly more nimbly).

GET MORE VITAMIN D

No matter how many other things you are doing to be healthier—eating better, moving around more—if your vitamin D levels are low you'll still be at big risk for developing some of the most pervasive diseases. The optimal way to get more of it is to expose your skin to natural sunlight with no sunscreen for twenty minutes a day (just before your skin starts to turn a different shade); supplements can also help if you live in a climate where that sun exposure isn't possible year round.

USE SMALLER PLATES

If eating less is one of your goals, here's an easy way to do it: reach for the small plates. Why? Research has found that people serve themselves less food when they use smaller plates. It also helps promote the practice of taking only what you need. If you end up wanting more, you'll make a conscious choice instead of gobbling it down simply because it's there. As an added bonus, you'll have more room in your dishwasher.

PART FOUR

Show Love

There are no two ways about it—
love is more than just a feeling. It's a force that
compels us to be the best that we can be—
kinder, more compassionate, more giving, and
more forgiving. The tips in this chapter help
make you more openhearted. They will bring
you closer to your partner, your family, and
everyone in your tribe as well as the strangers
you encounter every day—and as pack animals,
we humans need all the connections we can
get. Ultimately, being more loving is how you
translate your efforts to be a better person into
making the world a better place; it expands the
focus and the benefit of your efforts to others.
That's powerful magic.

ADMIT YOUR MISSTEPS

Sure, it feels bad to let down someone you love, but avoiding the subject doesn't make it better. When you've done or said something you wish you hadn't, the best way to rectify it is to own up to it. "I messed up, and I'm sorry" can go a long way toward repairing the situation. It can also spare you from mentally raking yourself over the coals. Once you've owned your mistake, offer a plan or collaborate together on a way to make things right.

FORGIVE OTHERS THEIR MISTAKES

Forgiving others requires you to acknowledge their humanity and see their point of view even when you feel wronged, which is a true sign of empathy and maturity. You may or may not want to stay in a relationship, but either way, forgiveness will help set down the burden of that hurt. It sets you both free.

CHECK YOUR BODY LANGUAGE

You communicate with more than just your words—your body language is constantly broadcasting information to other people. Do you know what your typical postures and gestures are saying about you? An eye roll conveys irritation or dismissal, arms crossed over your chest implies a closed heart, and standing with hands on hips sends a message of power. Take stock of the impression you're giving and make sure it's the message you want to be sending.

RECOGNIZE YOUR OWN HARD-HEADEDNESS

Stubbornness can come in handy if you're trying to do something hard. But if you're holding fast to something because you hate to be wrong, you're likely to alienate people. This can be tough to do in the moment—but try to get some perspective on your stubbornness. If you have to have the last word, are motivated by proving other people wrong, or do what you want regardless of what other people think, you're prioritizing hardheadedness over openheartedness. What trait do you want to lead with?

☐ TAKE ONE FOR THE TEAM

You can't win 'em all. Meaning, every once in a while, do what's best for the group, even if it's not what you want to do. You won't win any points for martyrdom, so don't overdo it. But when you concede with the intention of being of service, you keep yourself humble and you make a deposit in the bank of good deeds.

☐ WITNESS WITHOUT FIXING

When someone you care about is going through something painful, one of the most powerful things you can do is simply let her know you're there, you care, and you're willing to listen. In other words, bear witness to her struggles. It can be hard to resist the urge to want to fix things, but that's really not your role—your job is to help the other person know she isn't alone and support her if she needs it.

COEXIST PEACEFULLY

Some of our greatest change agents, including Martin Luther King Jr. and Gandhi, were proponents of nonviolence, which espouses peaceful action and thought even in the midst of conflict. As King described it, "You not only refuse to shoot a man, but you refuse to hate him." In this era of divisive politics, there are innumerable opportunities to vilify people on the other side of the aisle. Instead, consider ways in which you can peacefully interact with others when you disagree with them.

EXAMINE YOUR BROKEN PROMISES

It's not pleasant to think about how you may have let someone down, but it's a great way to gain insight into your own motives, which may be unclear to you. Think about a promise that you didn't keep. What was at the root? Was it people-pleasing, trying to look good, ignoring your inner wisdom? You're not looking for a reason to feel bad about yourself, but for insight that will help you evolve.

☐ ASK FOR FEEDBACK

Opening yourself up to criticism is a scary proposition—so scary that it may make you avoid any opportunity to get outside opinions on how you're doing. Which is a shame, because feedback can provide the objectivity you need to identify your blind spots and work through them. It takes courage to ask for someone else's observations of you, but it's hard to grow without them.

☐ CULTIVATE TRANSPARENCY

Constantly editing what you're going to say before you say it is draining. The majority of the time, what you're already thinking is perfectly good. If you feel funny about revealing your unedited thoughts, you can preface it with, "In the name of transparency..." Being real with people is liberating, and it creates more opportunities for true connection.

LISTEN BETTER

Good listening requires more than being quiet while the other person speaks. It takes focus (taking in what the other person is saying instead of rehearsing your response), curiosity (asking follow-up questions to get a clearer understanding), and empathy (validating the emotions you hear the other person expressing). And it probably goes without saying—but we can all use more reminders—putting down your phone or closing your computer is key.

ASK MORE AND BETTER QUESTIONS

Being inquisitive is a hallmark of being a good friend or partner—it shows you're interested in the other person. Questions that elevate a discussion tend to be: open-ended ("What do you think is a good way to proceed?"), nonleading ("How was it?" instead of "Did you have a good time?"), nonjudgmental ("What happened?" instead of "How did this get messed up?"), or thought-provoking ("Is there another way to think about this?").

ASK BEFORE YOU OFFER ADVICE

How much do you like it when someone gives you advice that you didn't ask for? Exactly. You may have a helpful idea, but if the other person doesn't want to hear it, offering it will fall on deaf ears and may even alienate you. Instead, change the dynamic by asking if the other person wants your advice: "I have an idea that I think might be helpful. Would you like to hear it?" If the answer is yes, you have the other person's attention and buy-in. If the answer is no, keep it to yourself.

STOP WORRYING ABOUT THE PEOPLE YOU LOVE

Chronic worriers often say, "I worry because I care." But while you may have a loving intention, worrying about another person is anything but productive. In fact, it's disempowering and broadcasts the message that you don't think the other person can handle whatever she is facing. Whether you express it in words or simply with your demeanor, your worry is not helping. It may take all the strength you have, but challenge yourself to set it aside.

GIVE ONE COMPLIMENT A DAY

It feels great to be recognized for doing something good. Pay that good feeling forward by giving more compliments. Whether you tell your partner that you appreciate the breakfast he made or you thank the cashier at the grocery store for her cheerful help, pointing out something specific and positive creates good feelings for them and for you. Making it a daily habit builds up the force field of good vibes even further.

STRENGTHEN YOUR EMPATHY MUSCLES

Empathy is being able to imagine how another person feels, and it's the foundation of meaningful relationships. Despite the fact that it's not often taught, empathy is also a skill that can be strengthened. Practice it by getting curious about strangers, asking questions, and seeking to understand the points of view and experiences of others. Building your empathy quotient will help you lead with your heart.

☐ SEND LOVING KINDNESS INSTEAD

Instead of worrying about a loved one, try a simple loving-kindness meditation. Sitting quietly with eyes closed, call up an image of the person in your mind. Silently repeat, "May you be happy. May you be free from suffering. May you be at peace." Continue for a few minutes. This practice helps you send positive energy that person's way. (For extra bonus points, repeat the same phrases toward yourself to help alleviate any worries that are self-directed.)

☐ LIGHTEN YOUR TONE

The content of your words are important, but the tone of your voice matters just as much, if not more. Why? Because "What a nice day" said with lightness carries a completely different message than "What a nice day" said with a sarcastic edge. You may think you're saying something kind, but if your tone is hard, your message will be misinterpreted. It's not just what you say that matters; it's also how you say it.

☐ LEARN HOW TO FORGIVE

Forgiveness is crucial for moving past a difficult time, but what if you just can't summon it? You may not be able to forgive the entire transgression, but maybe you can forgive one part of it, no matter how tiny. It will help unburden you of some of the hurt. To do it, complete this sentence: "I forgive him (or her) for..., and I hope to be able to forgive him (or her) for...one day soon."

☐ GET BETTER AT HAVING DIFFICULT CONVERSATIONS

Bringing up a touchy subject can be scary. But having that tough conversation is actually a bonding opportunity—if you can be present with each other and communicate how you're feeling, your relationship will be stronger. Start by inviting the other person to participate, and then focus on relating *your* experience, not what you think the other person is thinking: "I'd like to talk about something, do you have a few minutes?" And when they agree to have the talk, begin with, "Lately I've been feeling upset when I look at our bank balance, like my stomach has dropped to the floor, and I start getting scared about our financial future." Then ask them to share how they feel about the subject. Drawing on your empathy to see the situation from the other person's point of view and pointing out places where you agree will help you hear each other.

GIVE WHAT YOU WANT TO RECEIVE

Let's say you're feeling unappreciated at home. You could get upset and focus on all the ways you're taken for granted. But then you'd be compounding the problem. Instead, try showing more appreciation for yourself and for other people as well. It may seem counterintuitive, but you've got to give to get. You'll be surprised how much positive energy you get back when you send it out to others.

LEARN FROM YOUR DIFFICULT CONVERSATIONS

After you've had that difficult conversation (congratulations!), it's important to do a little postmortem analysis. How do you feel about how it went? How did you do getting across the points you wanted to make? What do you wish had happened differently? It will help you process and move forward, and it will also help you prepare for the next tough conversation (because we are never done having them).

STOP KEEPING SCORE

I cooked dinner, so he should do the dishes. I called last time, so it's her turn now. It's understandable to want the division of labor in a relationship to be equitable, but keeping track of who did what for sake of "fairness" can backfire, because a good relationship is not about winning and losing. It's about communicating, asking, giving, receiving, and compromising. Stop keeping score, and you'll both come out ahead.

LOOK FOR THE WIN-WIN

A great place to focus that's not about keeping score is looking for the win-win. By finding the approach that allows everyone to gain something, you challenge yourself to think differently, look for opportunity, and keep the other person's needs top of mind (right alongside your own). It makes the sometimes hard work of being in a relationship feel more like a shared adventure.

☐ OFFER EXPLANATIONS, NOT EXCUSES

The next time you goof up, resist the urge to make an excuse and instead offer a simple explanation. The difference here is subtle, but important. An excuse lays blame ("I didn't write you back because my boss has heaped so much work on me"), while an explanation fills in blanks ("I've been in a crunch time at work and thus not paying as much attention to my inbox"). It's an empowering shift.

☐ HELP OUT WITHOUT OVEREXTENDING YOURSELF

Of course you want to be able to help friends and family when they're in need, but what if you don't have a ton of time to commit? Keep in mind that the help doesn't have to come from your own hands to be helpful. Listening and empathizing can go a long way. So can connecting them to a book, class, group, or particular person for more support. Let this knowledge help you let go of the guilt.

□ EMBRACE VULNERABILITY

It's nice to be well regarded by colleagues, friends, and loved ones, but presenting only the things that make you look good keeps people at bay. Being open about mistakes, messes, and goof-ups only make you more relatable and lovable. People recognize truth when they see it and hear it; share more of yours and you'll attract the people who appreciate it and repel those who don't (these are probably people you don't want to be all that close to anyway).

□ DISAGREE BETTER

Every relationship has its share of disagreements. The trick is to learn how to disagree well. A simple principle that's taught in comedy improv—the "yes, and" technique—can help. When someone says something you don't agree with, don't discount what the other person is saying by using words such as *no* or *but*. Instead, validate what the other person is saying (*yes*) and then offer a solution that builds on it (*and*). It helps you collaborate on a solution that incorporates both your points of view.

☐ STOP TRYING TO FIX OTHERS

You may have a well-honed ability to see what's not working and devise a solution, but applying that skill to other people can be troublesome. What you see as helpful problem-solving is likely to make the other person feel defensive to the point where nothing you say can penetrate. Save your problem-solving for filing taxes or streamlining a process at work. When it comes to people, aim to be more of a support-giver. Often, people are simply looking for someone to listen and commiserate with them.

☐ ADMIT WHAT YOU DON'T KNOW

Nobody enjoys looking foolish, and so we tend to hide confusion or ignorance. But saying things like "I don't know the answer to that," "I'm not familiar with what you're talking about," or "I'm confused" relieves you of the need to present yourself a certain way, which frees you up to stay present in the conversation. It's another way to embrace vulnerability in the moment, which fosters connection and empathy—key components of every productive discussion.

PAUSE FOR THE CAUSE

When you're at a loss for words, remember you can always pause long enough to take a breath—that tiny little vacation from talking is typically enough to allow you to access what you're really trying to convey. Let your inspiration be to respond instead of react. And when you truly don't know what to say, all you ever have to do is relate what you're feeling and experiencing (instead of feeling pressure to come up with the perfect comeback).

LEARN YOUR LOVER'S LANGUAGE

There's no guarantee that the person you're in a relationship with appreciates the same displays of love that you do. Rather than let this be a source of disconnect, use a combination of asking and observing to determine what your partner likes. Does he prefer love notes? Gifts? Kind acts? Sweet talk? Physical displays of affection? Your styles don't have to match if you each feel that your needs are being met.

START A MEANINGFUL TRADITION

Rituals are an important way of processing emotions and marking the passage of time. Creating your own meaningful traditions with your family or circle of friends brings you together and gives you something to look forward to as a group. Whether it's daily (naming things you're grateful for over dinner), quarterly (making a list of seasonal goals), or annually (a New Year's Day walk), establishing a ritual will draw the ones who are close to you even closer.

GET BETTER AT VALIDATING

Everyone has a fundamental need to feel heard by loved ones, yet not everyone is skilled at validating others' feelings. To help another person feel accepted, say, "I can understand why you're feeling *x*" (use the other person's word to make sure you get it right), or "That sounds like it must have been intense," or "I can see this means a lot to you." You're not necessarily agreeing with what the other person is saying, you're simply hearing and accepting your loved one's experience. It's small, but it's powerful.

GET OBJECTIVE HELP WHEN YOU NEED IT

Every relationship needs a little outside assistance from time to time—whether it's a nugget of parenting advice you get from a book or insight you get from a therapist. Feeling like you should be able to figure out everything on your own is isolating and can keep you from getting the help you need to feel better.

STAY CURIOUS WHEN YOU'RE FURIOUS

Everyone gets steamed from time to time, and generally this furious feeling is accompanied by a strong sense of being right—or, conversely, having been wronged. But if you can manage to ask yourself some questions in the midst of that heated feeling (such as, *What exactly is getting me so upset? What if there's another way to interpret this? What if this really has nothing to do with me?*), it is more likely that you will be able to see a way out.

LEARN HOW TO REPAIR
AFTER A FIGHT

Quarrels happen. While you can learn to disagree better, there's still one more step to take when the squabble is through, and that's to learn how to repair the relationship. Use the phrases "I understand you're feeling...," "I'm sorry for...," and "In the future I will..." to validate the other person, own your role, and make a plan to avoid revisiting this particular fight in the future. Your bond will be stronger for it.

UP YOUR ODDS OF
BEING HELPFUL

When someone you care about is going through a rough patch it can be hard to know what to do to help. A basic option that we often forget is simply to ask, "How can I help you?" After that, take her suggestions to heart, but have a specific option or two of your own on hand in case she says she doesn't know: "I could call to check in with you a couple of times a week. Does that sound good?" Having a clear action plan helps keep awkwardness at bay.

CUDDLE MORE

Snuggling with someone you love does more than just make you feel good; it also soothes your nervous system and releases feel-good hormones that promote your physical health and mental well-being. (Cozying up to pets totally counts.) Don't be shy about asking for the nuzzles you need—after all, those beneficial side effects will kick in for the person (or pet) you're snuggling with too.

JUST SAY NO TO GHOSTING

If it's time to break up with someone—a romantic interest or a friend—resist the urge to simply never call again. You don't have go into detail, but do the other person the favor of knowing where things stand. It can be as simple as, "I'm sorry, this isn't working out for me. Good luck." The pain of hearing it's over heals faster than the confusion and betrayal that comes from wondering what happened.

☐ PRIORITIZE INTIMACY

Different relationships serve different purposes—you may have a friend who's great for goofing off with but the connection may not go much deeper than that. Just be sure that you do have some relationships where you can share your innermost thoughts without fear of judgment. This level of emotional intimacy deepens your understanding of yourself and the other person; it also opens your heart and makes you equipped to be a better participant in all your relationships.

☐ ACCEPT THAT DISAGREEMENTS ARE BOUND TO HAPPEN

The thought of continually being in perfect sync with all the important people in your life may sound idyllic, but it's simply not realistic. Disagreements are bound to happen. Accepting that can help you deal with arguments more skillfully. Rather than taking the fact that you're having a fight as a bad omen, you can focus on understanding and collaborating on the issue at hand.

OWN YOUR ROLE

When having a disagreement, a quick and powerful way to defuse some of the tension is to admit how you contributed to the situation. For example, if your partner is irritated that you don't seem to be listening, say, "I was trying to finish something up and not giving you my full attention, and I'm sorry for that." It doesn't mean you should take 100 percent responsibility for the whole situation—taking the entire blame discounts the other person's role.

RECOGNIZE THAT EVERYONE IS ON HER OWN PATH

When someone you care about is going through a hard time but is resistant to help, remember that every person on the planet is on her own journey. Perhaps the difficulty she's experiencing is exactly what she needs to learn the lesson that will help her grow. Your interference or minimization of the difficulty she is facing could prevent her from getting the lesson. Certainly, ask how you can help and share how you care, but take care not to meddle.

BE A COUPLE OF COLLABORATORS

Power struggles don't have to be a mainstay of your relationship. Make it your intention to cocreate a life by collaborating instead of manipulating. Share your hopes and dreams, and ask your partner to share his. Then look for the places where your desires intersect instead of how they differ. It takes more effort and it requires more compromises, but the harmony it creates is worth it.

OFFER YOUR PRESENCE

Now that we have more distractions than ever, it's more important than ever that we make the effort to be fully present during our interactions with people we care about. Put down the phone, close the computer, turn off the television, lay down the newspaper, and give someone the gift of your full attention. The fact that this kind of focused personal attention is rare makes it all the more powerful.

GIVE YOUR PARTNER SPECIAL TREATMENT

It's so easy to get lulled into taking your partner for granted—he's already committed to you, after all. But little inconsiderations can add up to big feelings of disconnect. What are some things you know your partner would love? Put your socks in the hamper? Be ready to go five minutes early? Try doing one thing a day just because you know he'll like it. Treating others how you'd like to be treated elevates your relationship.

STOP TRYING TO KEEP THE PEACE

Aiming to not ruffle others' feathers seems like a noble aim, but it's not always the highest good. Your efforts are based on your judgment of what's best—and you may not always have enough information to know what a situation needs. There are times when hearing an upsetting truth is exactly what a person or situation needs to attain clarity. Make it your intention to be able to discern when to avoid making waves and when to let the tide do what it will.

WRITE MORE LETTERS

Once upon a time, we all wrote letters to each other—pages of newsy updates and secret confessions that made you feel like you'd spent quality time with someone even though the other person was far away. In this digital age, sending something handwritten in the mail makes a huge impression on the recipient. As a happy side effect, the more letters you write, the more you'll receive back. You may find that writing things out in longhand helps crystallize your thinking too.

LEAVE A LOVE NOTE IN THE CEREAL BOX

As nice as it to tell the people you love that you love them, it's important to demonstrate your affection too, instead of only expressing it verbally. It could be the tiniest thing—like leaving your loved one a nice note ("I think you're great") in the cereal box or on a Post-it on his steering wheel. The element of surprise gives a sweet gesture even more impact.

☐ WHEN YOU'RE THINKING OF SOMEONE, LET HER KNOW

It's so easy to think about someone fondly, consider reaching out to her, and then quickly dismiss it because something else is more pressing. When someone crosses your mind—you remember something the two of you laughed about or you wonder how she is—act on that inspiration before it fades. You could send a text, social media message, postcard, voice mail, or letter. It doesn't take much time or effort to act on that impulse, and it yields big rewards.

☐ PURSUE SHARED INTERESTS

You don't have to like all the same things that your partner does, but find one or two activities that you both enjoy. Spending time together doing something that you both find rewarding is a great bonding opportunity and gives you shared memories to draw on in the future. It may take some trial and error to find one, or to replace one that no longer does the trick, but keep trying; the closeness it creates is worth it.

☐ DON'T WAIT TO GET WHAT YOU NEED

Instead of waiting for your loved ones to intuit your needs and provide them without prompting, take responsibility for fulfilling your own needs—or asking for help if you aren't able to meet them yourself. Otherwise you could be waiting a long time, slowly building resentment, while your basic needs go unmet. And why would you choose that? The choice is yours, and there's no shame in being honest about what you need, with yourself and with other people.

☐ PRAISE LOUDLY, CORRECT QUIETLY

Good elementary school teachers know that you elicit better behavior when you acknowledge kids for doing things right rather than only calling them out when they do things wrong. The same is true for people of all ages. When someone you love does something that makes you happy, be generous with your appreciation. And when someone does something that doesn't sit well with you, share that quietly. Put another way: thank more, nag less.

PLAN FOR NO PLANS

As important as shared activities can be, it's also important to spend time together that doesn't require hustling or schedules. To make sure it happens, carve out a chunk of time—say, Sunday mornings—when no plans are allowed. Knowing you have scheduled downtime will help you stay grounded during any hectic spurts that happen other days of the week. It doesn't mean you have to stay home—it just means that you'll have some space for spontaneity.

DON'T BE A SNOWPLOW

When it comes to helping the people you love deal with adversity, are you more like a snowplow—aiming to remove every single obstacle—or like a salt truck—giving just enough assistance to help prevent full-blown wipeouts? If you suspect you may be snowplowing, ask yourself, *How could I do less and still let my loved ones feel supported*? Check that you aren't imposing your desire for control onto other people.

☐ GIVE A BETTER COMPLIMENT

Not all compliments are created equally. Praising traits, such as "You're so smart" or "You are such a nice person," can make the recipient feel as if he *always* has to display that quality or else he's falling short. Instead, compliment specific actions: "I can tell you gave this a lot of thought," or "That was so generous of you." Giving your praise context helps it do what you intended—to give the other person a nice lift.

☐ TAKE AN INTEREST IN YOUR LOVED ONE'S PASSIONS

You may be married to a sports nut and have no interest in football. Or have a child who loves video games that only baffle you. You don't have to start painting your face and tailgating, but taking an interest and asking questions shows you care about the person, even if you don't care about the subject. Not displaying any interest implies that you disapprove.

LET DOWN YOUR GUARD

When someone you care about gives you negative feed-back, do you take it in or take it personally? It's not easy to hear criticism directed at you, but if you immediately put up your shields and get defensive (raising your voice, justifying, countering with criticisms of your own) you perpetuate disconnection, and that feels just as bad as being critiqued.

STOP WAITING TO BE ASKED

In your relationships, do you initiate plans or wait to be asked? Do you proactively bring up a sensitive topic or wait for a triggering event? Be brave enough to go first—share how you're feeling before there's an upset and reach out to the friend you've been out of touch with. You don't always have to be the proactive one, but don't always be the passive one either.

PART FIVE

Give Back

Giving back is about more than
being virtuous—it's about caring more,
believing in your power to do good, and creating positive changes in your community and
in the world at large. The funny paradox about
giving back is that it feels *really* good to help
others, and those good feelings help energize
you to do more and inspire others to do it too.

The tips in this chapter help you find
ways to help others that suit you perfectly and
that don't require you to overextend yourself,
all while having a big impact.

☐ THINK ABOUT YOUR LEGACY

What do you want to be remembered for? Something you instilled in your kids? A value you perpetuated? An organization or cause you supported? These are big questions, but you do have models: think about the institutions, people, and organizations you support, that benefit you, and that you value and appreciate. How can you do your part to help those things carry on? A generation from now, maybe someone will be looking to your example to shape her own legacy, but only if you act.

☐ USE YOUR POWER FOR GOOD

You have more power than you can contemplate. While you often don't consider it as you live your life, every thought you have and every move you make has an effect in your own life and in the lives of others. Periodically asking yourself, "How can I use my power for good?" is a gut-check that reminds you of your own agency and keeps you focused on using your influence with intention and purpose. Pay a compliment to the checkout clerk at the grocery store who's clearly having a bad day, stand up and ask the unspoken question at the neighborhood association meeting, vote with your conscience instead of your party—there are numerous ways to exercise your power in a positive way if you look for them. Do more of it and you'll create ripples that empower others to do it too.

SEEK TO UNDERSTAND COMPLEX PROBLEMS

It's difficult to use your power for good if you don't have an understanding of what's going on around you. If you discern a problem that you want to help address—whether it's something big, like prison reform, or something smaller scale, like the homework policy at your child's school—your first step is to educate yourself. Read articles or books, talk to a couple of people who are involved first-hand, show up to meetings where the issue is discussed. You may not be able to grasp every nuance or learn everything there is to learn—that could take a lifetime. But being informed is key to making decisions from a wise—as opposed to a reactive—place.

MAKE GIVING A HABIT

Giving of what we have is helpful, and it feels good. An easy way to do more of it is to find ways to make the process more automatic. Become a sustaining member of your favorite organizations and sign up to make a recurring payment—even a small amount every month makes a big difference. Write checks to charitable causes on the same day you pay your bills. Keep a laundry basket at the bottom of your closet to collect unwanted items—when it's full, drop it off at your local thrift shop. When you make giving back a no-brainer, you'll do more of it.

FIND THE RIGHT MATCH
FOR YOUR GIFTS

There are so many opportunities to get involved, so many places and causes that need help, but not every opportunity to help is a good match for you. When you're investigating a potential volunteer role, take the time to investigate what the organization truly needs. Is it a match for what you have to offer? If yes, talk to someone there: "Here's what I think I can contribute. Does that sound like it would be helpful?" Getting buy-in—on both sides—before you go all-in makes it more likely that you'll feel restored by your efforts, instead of frustrated and depleted.

TRAVEL MORE

Travel helps you learn new things and make lasting memories. It also opens your heart and mind to people who live differently than you do. And the benefits of travel don't end when you return. Visiting other places helps you see your home with new eyes, which makes you more appreciative of it and therefore more likely to be engaged in life in your hometown. If you can't swing a long trip right now, head to the nearest city or town for a day. Sometimes just a day trip to the other side of town can bring unexpected rewards.

SOLVE A PROBLEM

If there's a problem that you find yourself complaining about repeatedly, take steps to solve it. If people drive too fast down your street, for example, talk to the city about installing a speed bump. Know that even if you don't affect a complete remedy, your caring and your actions are likely to be heard. Of course, some problems are intractable and sometimes our efforts come to naught—but even in these cases, you will be proud of doing your part and acting on behalf of your interests and those of others.

BLESS THEIR HEARTS

If there are people who are frustrating, disappointing, or annoying you, there's a simple phrase that can help you soften to them: "Bless your heart." Repeating this Southern phrase, whether out loud or silently to yourself, helps you think better of the person who's otherwise bugging you. It may not evaporate all the irritation you're feeling, but it lessens it to the point that you can act more kindly.

SPEAK UP WHEN YOU SEE INJUSTICE

When someone is being wronged, it's much too common for onlookers to go into a mild state of shock and say nothing. Maybe it's a person of color getting poor service at a restaurant, or a kid being taunted at the neighborhood park, or a fan of the other team getting heckled at a sporting event. Or it could be something less public—a male coworker getting a promotion over a female coworker who is more deserving, for example. Whatever it is, consider this your reminder to show your solidarity with others. You can either call out the offending party by publicly acknowledging the troubling behavior or have a private conversation with the person to address it. Just as importantly, check in with the person who's been offended if you can. Ask, "Are you okay?" and "How can I help?" We can all get better at having each other's backs.

VOTE WITH YOUR BALLOT

People fought and died so that you could have the right to vote for one simple reason: your vote is an expression of your voice, and your voice matters. If you already vote, good for you! Your work now is to help encourage other people to do the same.

☐ KEEP RAISING YOUR CONSCIOUSNESS

To be alive is to be dynamic. Your cells are constantly rebuilding themselves. The only part of you that doesn't automatically renew is your thoughts—in fact, they can stagnate if you don't challenge them. Have more conversations with people who think differently than you do. Read books about people whose lives are different from yours. Keep seeking to understand more about your fellow humans—we need all the enlightened thinkers we can get.

☐ VOTE WITH YOUR DOLLARS

Giving money to charities you care about is important, but you also support causes through your everyday purchasing decisions. By buying Fair Trade coffee, for example, you help ensure that coffee growers make a living wage. Giving more thought to the things you buy and the companies you buy from can make a big impact on the quality of life for people all over the world. There's more to life than the bottom line: let your spending reflect your values.

SAY "THANK YOU" MORE

Thanking someone is more than just being polite—it's an opportunity to connect and to honor something meaningful that happened between the two of you, whether it was big or small. Mix up the ways you offer your thanks. A handwritten note, with a specific and sincere message, makes a big impression, as does a phone call or voice mail message. You don't have to jump through hoops; a sincere verbal "thank you" in the moment can be all it takes. However you choose to communicate your gratitude, just be sure you do.

LOOK PEOPLE IN THE EYE

Meeting another person's gaze is a powerful way to connect. It's intimate, yes, but the discomfort of vulnerability quickly dissolves into a warm, connected feeling. We are all descended from the same handful of ancestors, living on the same planet, and when you look someone else in the eye, you remember that connection. It makes you feel both seen and valued and it can go a long, long way toward healing what otherwise might feel like an uncrossable divide.

☐ DON'T AVOID THE UNCOMFORTABLE CONVERSATIONS

When you hear of a friend or acquaintance who has lost a loved one or who is facing a health crisis, you likely want to reach out and offer support, but may hesitate if you're not sure what to say. It's natural and honorable to want to reach out in the right way, but don't let not knowing the best way to do it prevent you from doing something. If you're unsure of a good approach, ask a friend who has been through a similar situation. Or simply be honest: "I'm thinking about you and would like to help. What can I do?"

☐ COME BEARING GIFTS

When someone invites you to her house, whether for a meal or a longer stay, bring a small gift. It can be something that will contribute to your time together— a bottle of wine or breakfast fixings—or something meaningful to your host, like a bouquet of her favorite flowers (preferably in a simple vase so she won't have to tend to them right away). Even those of us who remember to bring gifts to homes we're visiting for the first time often forget to do it for the hosts who mean the most to us: our closest friends and family. Yes, Dad and Mom too. Acknowledge the effort and thoughtfulness your host is extending, and you'll set the stage for even more enjoyment—by everyone— during the time you spend together.

☐ ENCOURAGE PEOPLE

When a friend or loved one shares news about a new endeavor, take care to say something support-ive, even if you doubt the wisdom of his choice or his ability to see it through. Sharing new plans takes courage. Even a simple "really?" from you can trig-ger a wave of second-guessing. You don't have to support every decision your friends and loved ones make, but get in the habit of supporting them at the start. You can share your thoughts once the endeavor is underway, if they ask for them.

☐ MAKE FRIENDS WITH SOMEONE OUTSIDE YOUR DEMOGRAPHIC

It's easy to travel in familiar circles, but it's hard to know how to connect with others if you only social-ize within a bubble of people who are similar to you. Be open to relationships with people of different ages, ethnicities, professions, and backgrounds than you. You can meet them through work, at network-ing events, by becoming more active in civic organ-izations or local charities, at Meetup groups, or in continuing-education classes—the opportunities are everywhere once you start to look for them. When you do, you'll broaden your understanding of the world, which will help you be a more informed and thoughtful participant in it. Be bold, and open your world to someone with whom you appear to have lit-tle in common.

☐ HELP A CRYING BABY'S MOTHER

No one gets excited to hear a baby crying, especially when on a crowded flight or other situation where there is no way to escape it. You can bemoan your fate and get angry, or you can offer to help—because the baby's caretaker is likely struggling in that moment. You don't have to be a magical baby whisperer; even if all you do is choose to quietly send some positive feelings to the child, or give a look of encouragement from across the aisle, it will help everyone feel calmer.

☐ ACTUALLY SILENCE YOUR PHONE

There's no denying it—mobile phones have become an essential part of our daily lives. So essential that you may hesitate or forget to turn off the ringer. But there are still places where being away from noisy technology is not only nice, it's a necessary part of the experience. Be the person who actually turns off your cell phone at the movies, the theater, and yoga class so that everyone who has paid good money to have an immersive, transporting experience can have it—including you.

GO ON IMPRESSIONS, NOT ASSUMPTIONS

One way to be more giving is to make fewer assumptions about other people, which are generally fairly judgmental and often incorrect. Rather, aim to gather an impression of the other person. What does her eye contact, body language, and overall state of being communicate? Forming an impression requires you to be observant and receptive and can keep you from getting stuck in a knee-jerk reaction.

CHOOSE YOUR CAUSES

It can be overwhelming to decide how to get involved in giving back. To narrow your choices and find a good match, consider what you care most about. Boil it down to two or three causes that move you the most and focus your efforts there. No one person can give as much as is needed to everyone who needs it, so let go of any guilt of not helping more. You don't need to do it all, you just need to do your part. If we all did that, the impact would be huge.

USE A GIVING MANTRA

When in doubt about how to give back, make it your mantra to be of service. You're not looking for the "right" thing to do—it's easy to get stuck in trying to figure out what the exact right thing is. Look for the helpful thing. It helps shift your attention away from feeling like there's nothing that could possibly help, or feeling upset that there's so much that needs to be done. If you aren't sure what would be useful, ask, "How can I be of help?"

EXTEND INVITATIONS

When you find the cause you want to devote some time to, invite your friends and family members to join you. It's a great way to bring even more man-power to the cause. And the people around you would probably like to do more things to give back, but maybe haven't had the time to figure out the what, where, and when. Your invitation makes it easy for them to get involved, which means you're provid-ing a service to them too. Best of all, bringing your friends and family along when you give time doubles your efforts.

☐ TAKE CARE OF THE LITTLE GUY

As important as it is to seek to improve your circumstances, you also want to reach back and extend a hand to someone who is in a tougher spot than you are. But that can be tricky—for some of us, a voice tends to kick in once we get what we wanted, telling us we have to guard it against those who would take it from us. Be prudent, but don't listen too closely to that voice—the more generous you are, the more life gives back to you. Helping folks who have less than you will help you stay compassionate, grateful, and generous. This could mean financial support—such as giving to a scholarship fund—but it could also mean offering guidance—by becoming a big sister, or volunteering at a school, or mentoring new business owners through a local entrepreneurial incubator. Sharing the benefits you've managed to accrue will help you and the people you're helping feel more connected and accomplished.

☐ DRESS UP

When you make plans to meet up with other people— a job interview, a coffee, a double date—dress up a little bit. It's not to impress the other person; it's to show respect and communicate that you value the other person's time and attention—that getting together with that person, whatever the reason, is an occasion, and you want to look your best. It's not likely to hurt, is it? Also, when you give respect, you're more likely to get it back.

TAKE CARE OF ANIMALS

You don't always have to give back to other people—animals need care and support too, and tending to them is fairly uncomplicated. Many animals give a ton of affection and companionship in return. Even if you don't want to take on the responsibility of adopting a pet, you can offer to dog- or cat-sit, foster animals until they find a forever home, or volunteer at a local shelter.

GET TO KNOW YOUR NEIGHBORS

You may not be best friends with your neighbors, but having a social relationship with them makes a neighborhood feel more like a community. Drop off a bottle of wine when new neighbors move in, host a potluck dinner or holiday party for the people who live on your street or in your building, or check in on older neighbors during inclement weather—all these little gestures add up to a big web of support that benefits everyone.

LOOK FOR THE QUICK HIT

A common—and sensible—reason for not doing more to give back is not having the time. But not everything requires hours. It only takes a minute to buy an extra jar of peanut butter for the food drive at your child's school, for example, to drop off a bag of books you no longer read to the local library, or to patronize a store that donates a percentage of its profits. Every little thing you do counts.

GIVE MORE WITHOUT GIVING TOO MUCH

It's perfectly okay to pitch in at a level that makes sense for you—there are no bonus points for giving till it hurts. If the PTA requires too much of a time commitment, can you share your position or role with another person? If you only have a limited budget for donating, can you make it during a matching grant to make your dollars go further? Or if you can't make the event, can you share a post on *Facebook* asking for volunteers? When you find ways to give back that feel good to you, you'll find more ways to do it.

LET OTHERS GO FIRST

When you're in a hurry it's easy to wish everyone would just get out of your way already. To pull yourself out of that subconscious "me first" state of mind, make it a point to let other people go before you—pause to let a pedestrian cross, or let the other driver make a left turn, or allow the other folks on the elevator to get off first. Being in public is not an obstacle course: remember that you're sharing space, and act like it. Doing this will help you get more comfortable with being patient and with occasionally putting others' needs before your own.

☐ ASK HOW SOMEONE IS DOING

When you're checking out at the grocery store, filling up the car with gas, or picking up books from the library, take a moment to ask how the person who's waiting on you is doing. After all, you need to interact with this person anyway—taking the tiny extra step of asking how the person is doing and listening for the answer can be a lovely little communal moment in the midst of mundane tasks.

☐ GIVE MORE POSITIVE REVIEWS

With the rise of the Internet and social media, customer reviews are more important than ever to businesses of all types. Leave more reviews for positive experiences than for negative ones. In fact, it's better to mention a bad experience to a manager first so he has a chance to make it right. Refrain from leaving bad reviews if you haven't taken this step. Make it your aim to reward the folks who are doing it right more than to punish folks who get it "wrong."

SHARE RESOURCES

You don't always have to do the heavy lifting of showing up or pulling out your checkbook to give back—sometimes all it takes is a social media share (ideally with a personal note to explain why you recommend supporting this cause) to provide meaningful support. People pay more attention to things their friends recommend—use that social currency for good.

BE THE VOICE OF REASON

One way to give back is to take a stand against pettiness. If you're in a crowd of people who are gossiping, be the person who points out another way of interpreting the events, or say something nice about the person being discussed. You don't have to scold anyone; keep your tone light and simply offer an alternative point of view. If that doesn't work, change the subject or excuse yourself. Taking energy away from the conversation will take away some of its power.

☐ MAKE IT PERSONAL

When you donate things, whether it's a check or a piece of clothing, leave a personal touch. A note in a coat pocket or a hand-drawn design on the back of an envelope leaves a lasting impression on the person who receives it and reminds you both that it's not just about the money or the things—it's about people helping people.

☐ DEFUSE ROAD RAGE

Road rage is real—it happens to everyone. But it doesn't have to be long-lasting. Imagining that the other person has just heard tragic news, for example, can help take the sting out of whatever wrong you may believe the person has committed. Or if you made the offensive move, raising your hands and eyebrows in the universal sign of *sorry!* can change everything. Of course, if you can see the rage on the other person's face, it's probably better not to engage. In that case, silently bless their heart as you keep moving.

STOCK A CLOSET WITH GIFTS

Here's a trick your grandmother may have employed: keep a few giftable items on hand to make giving a little token incredibly easy. Nobody likes getting an obviously impersonal gift, but certain items such as a box of pretty cards, a fancy bar of chocolate, or a packet of wildflower seeds are always appreciated. You can give them as thanks, or as encouragement, or for no particular reason at all.

SHORE UP OUR COLLECTIVE BACKBONE

Small businesses are more than just a feel-good story, they're the backbone of our economy—they provide half of the jobs in America. Make it a point to patronize your locally owned businesses, support them on social media, and tell your friends about the businesses you love. Word of mouth is the most powerful marketing there is, and when local businesses thrive, we all thrive.

LEAVE LOVE NOTES IN PUBLIC PLACES

Getting an unexpected positive message can put a spring in your step for a whole day. Give that gift to others by leaving a love note in a public place—a sticky note on a bathroom mirror that says "You're gorgeous," for example, or a sign on a coffee shop bulletin board that says "You are so loveable."

☐ MAKE A HELPFUL INTRODUCTION

Being a thoughtful connector of people is incredibly rewarding—it's such a thrill to introduce two people who end up getting married, or to hook up a job-seeking friend with a contact whose company is hiring. You may not be able to be the person who provides the end goal, but you can certainly be the person who helps make the connection that leads to the end goal. So when a friend tells you what she's hoping to do, think, "Who do I know?"

☐ HOLD THE ELEVATOR

We've all been there—the elevator doors open when we're still ten steps away. Challenge yourself to be the stranger who holds the doors open to let someone else on. The simplest gestures can make such a big impression—make more of them and you can feel confident that you're creating positive ripples that extend well beyond that one little elevator.

PICK UP THAT POOP

Petting and snuggling with a dog is fun; picking up the poop is not. But poop is a fact of life, and picking it up is part of the responsibility that comes with caring for an animal. Ignoring it doesn't make it go away—it makes your mess someone else's bad day when he inadvertently steps in it. Whatever your version of dog poop—be it the food your kids dropped on the floor at restaurants, the trash in your car that you might be tempted to throw out the window, the late-night snack that ended up as crumbs on the couch—do everyone a favor and put it where it belongs. It's the right thing to do.

PICK UP THE LITTER

Sometimes the messes that need picking up aren't yours. You may not be the source of it, but if you see litter lying around, do what you can to address it. You don't have to clean the whole park, but you can pick up the food wrapper sitting right in the middle of the path. It only takes a few seconds, but it leaves things better than you found them. Therefore, it's a great use of your time, even though it's not technically your responsibility.

GET INVOLVED IN YOUR NEIGHBORHOOD

Feeling attached to your hometown is a boon for your personal happiness and satisfaction. And volunteering boosts your mood, wards off depression, and even makes you physically healthier. Combine these two feel-good activities by finding a way to give back close to home. Volunteer at the library, join the snow-shoveling brigade, attend the neighborhood association meetings, or volunteer to write for the local paper. When you do, you'll start to see more familiar friendly faces when you walk down the street.

BE A SOURCE OF LONG-TERM SUPPORT

As nice as it is to show up with a hot meal when people you care about become ill or lose a loved one, they need support long after the initial shock wears off. The best way to show your continuing support is to check in regularly, float invitations to talk more deeply (let her decide if and when she's ready), and offer to do something specific: "How about I pick up the kids from school one day this week," for example. Share a bit about what's going on in your own life so the relationship stays balanced. Don't let the fact that your life is continuing as normal color your perception that hers is too.

...AND PICK SOMETHING UP FOR THEM WHILE YOU'RE AT IT

Sometimes you legitimately may not have time to sit and visit with a sick relative or a friend with a new baby, but you can still be helpful by tying in something that helps them with things you're doing anyway. For example, cook a double recipe of chili and pack up half of it for your relative, or ask your friend what she needs at the store that you can pick up on your next grocery run. The fact that it's less time-intensive doesn't make it less helpful.

ASK WHAT SUPPORT MEANS TO THEM

While it's noble to want to give back, the people you want to give to are the experts on what they need—not you. To make your efforts more helpful, ask, "How can I support you?" If they don't know, you can be of service simply by asking the questions that help them name their need, such as: "What's something you're struggling with?" "If you could wave a magic wand and change one thing, what would it be?" "What would make your life a little easier?" Knowing that information will make your contributions cleaner and more effective.

START THE GROUP YOU'RE
LONGING FOR

If there's some group you'd love to join—the book club, the knitting bee, the neighborhood watch—but you can't seem to find one, start it. If it seems too daunting to take on alone, well, that's probably why no one's done it yet. Get a friend to do it with you! Consider this encouragement the sign that you've been waiting for to go ahead and make it happen. Don't let the fact that your "it" doesn't exist yet keep you from giving back.

GET ACTIVATED

Democracy is built on the idea that "the people" participate in it. And unless you are reading this in a foreign land with a different form of government, you are one of the "people." Consider this your reminder to put your voice and your efforts to use for the good of society at large. There are so many ways to get involved. Even if you only did one of these things once a quarter, it would make a huge difference: Help register people to vote, choose one issue you care about to follow and participate in, communicate with your local representatives (put their numbers in your phone so you can call them easily), show up at a town hall with your elected officials and share a personal story that pertains to an issue being discussed, put a sign in your yard for the candidate you support. Whatever effort you're able to do is welcomed, and needed. This land is your land too, after all.

PART SIX

Stay Committed

Deciding to make a difference is a wonderful thing and a vital step on any journey toward positive change. But it is only the first step. Change doesn't come simply from making up your mind; it's the result of doing things differently on a consistent basis. That's where a sense of commitment comes in.

The tips in this section will help you stay committed to making continual progress by keeping you in touch with your motivation, using your community to stay accountable, and keeping it fun. Best of all, these tips will help you get back on track when you lose momentum, which is bound to happen on any long-term endeavor, and to do it without beating yourself up.

☐ GO FOR CONSISTENCY OVER FREQUENCY

Committing to a new course of action may seem to demand a grand gesture: *I'm going to meditate for twenty minutes every day.* But if you miss a day, all can seem lost, so—if you're like most of us—you probably quit and tell yourself it's too hard. To up your odds of success, lower the bar: *I will sit on my meditation cushion at some point each day.* Some days you may only sit on that cushion for ten seconds; some days it will be twenty minutes. Either way, you're building your commitment muscles. More may be better, but some is always better than none.

☐ WRITE A MISSION STATEMENT

To help make choices that take you toward what you want rather than away from it, write a personal mission statement—a short paragraph that sums up what you hold dear. To write one, start with a few keywords that describe traits or values that are important to you, then weave them together to form a sentence or short paragraph. That way, when an opportunity comes along, you have a barometer to use as a decision-making guide.

BE A LIFELONG LEARNER

Like all humans, you have an innate curiosity. Keep it fed by continually exposing yourself to new ideas. That doesn't mean you have to enroll in a formal program, though you shouldn't rule it out. You can read books, watch *YouTube* videos, enroll in workshops, or ask someone to show you the ropes. If you have even more elaborate goals, consider that program you've always wanted to do. However you pursue new learning, doing so will keep opening up new swaths of the horizon and opening your mind to new possibilities.

SET GOALS YOU ACTUALLY WANT TO ACCOMPLISH

Goal-setting may seem like a responsible, proactive thing to do, and it absolutely can be, but if they're not the right goals it can be a form of self-sabotage. Making goals that sound good on paper but don't actually motivate you is setting yourself up for a strange kind of failure. And then, once your inner critic chimes in with "told you so," you become that much more likely to avoid setting the kinds of goals that will make a difference for you. Next time, ask what accomplishments would completely delight you. The only "good" goals are the ones that inspire you to action.

☐ CARE JUST A LITTLE BIT LESS ABOUT GETTING IT RIGHT

As honorable an intention as it is to want to get things absolutely perfect, it can also be a sneaky form of self-sabotage—if you have a great day of eating healthy foods but you end up having a piece of cake at a birthday party that evening, your inner critic might try to tell you that there's no point in trying to change the way you eat: *See? I told you this would never work. Pass the chips.* If you fall prey to thinking your efforts have to be perfect or else they are crap (and so many of us do), try making your barometer of success progress, not perfection.

☐ WASTE TIME WELL

If all your waking hours are spent doing the responsible thing, you will crash at some point. This isn't about being less committed or diligent; it's about living in balance. Just as you need conscious relaxation to counteract stress, you need goof-off time to stay productive. Rather than wasting time on scrolling through social media, find ways to "waste" time that will refresh your thinking—browsing a bookstore, going on a hike, or visiting a museum can all reboot your brain.

RETHINK HOW MUCH TIME YOU HAVE

Trying to find time for all the things you want to do in any given day can feel futile. But if you take a weekly view, you can see more possibility. There are 168 hours in a week—even if you work fifty hours and sleep for fifty-six, there are sixty-two hours left. That's no small helping! If you're telling yourself, *I don't have time for that*, what you're really saying is, *That's not a priority for me right now*. The time is there if you look.

ACT WHEN THE INSPIRATION STRIKES

Here's a typical scenario: You get the idea to work on your book idea, and then you think, *I don't have time right now.* Get better at ignoring that voice! Good things happen when you honor your inspirations. If you truly don't have time in that moment, at least get out your calendar and find a time when you can do it.

WOO YOUR CREATIVITY

Whenever you feel stuck or unproductive, it's time to change gears and put yourself in a physical environment that stimulates your thought process. The classic self-help tome *The Artist's Way* calls it an artist's date—going someplace that inspires your creativity, whether it's a fabric store, a spot in nature, or a movie. This is different from wasting time—this is about going out in search of inspiration, because your best thinking typically doesn't happen when you're sitting behind your desk.

FIND YOUR RHYTHM

Mapping out a regular routine for yourself can help you find the sweet spot between productivity and rest. Go to bed at roughly the same time every night, follow the same basic morning routine, commit to a couple of regular times during the week when you do the activities that help you feel your best. Special events can temporarily interrupt your schedule, and your rhythm will evolve over time, but that's okay. Creating a rhythm will help make your self-care a little more rote—just part of what you do every day—so that you free up energy and brain space for other things.

GET BETTER AT STARTING AGAIN

No matter how strong your commitment is, there will be times when you fall off the wagon. Depending on the project, it may happen daily. What some might label failure is actually a beautiful opportunity to be gentle with yourself—no internal tongue-lashings!—and just get started again. It's as simple as that. (And if it doesn't feel that simple, remember that you only have to do the one right next step to get in motion again; you don't have to map out the whole path or knock out a huge task to get back in the swing.) Getting back on track is one of the most important skills you can cultivate, so welcome any chance you get to hone it.

KEEP BETTER TRACK OF THE THINGS THAT MATTER

What you pay attention to tends to improve. So whatever change you're seeking to create, start tracking it. It can be high-tech—there are many gadgets that count your steps and/or monitor your sleep—or old-fashioned—a set of tally marks for every resume you send out, or a pen-and-paper food diary. It's not how you collect the information that matters; it's the chance to get an objective look at your progress that will inspire you to keep going.

CELEBRATE SEMI-COMPLETION

When you're going after something big—a new job, let's say—it may seem wise to postpone any celebrating until you've officially met your goal. But you don't know how long the process is going to take, and you want to keep your spirits up for the long haul. Keep track of each resume you send out, every contact you network with, and every interview you have, and every time you complete five steps, reward yourself. It will give you something positive to focus on instead of on the fact that you don't have the job—yet!

STAY THE COURSE

At some point, probably when you're in the midst of making some big and exciting change, something in your life may go haywire—your dishwasher breaks, your family member has a crisis, or maybe you even have a car accident. Resist the urge to read these events as a bad omen and view them instead as a test from the universe to see how committed you are. Whatever it is that's going cuckoo, pay it just as much attention as it needs, and no more. And then get back to creating what you are seeking to create.

☐ STRENGTHEN YOUR "KEEP GOING" MUSCLES

At some point, doing something that's important to you stops being fun and starts feeling hard. This is when it's so important to keep going, because moving forward despite the resistance you're feeling is purifying. It may feel pretty unpleasant to keep moving even though you want to quit, but it will pass. Maybe not as quickly as you'd like, but it will pass. Be undaunted. Keep thinking of how good it will feel on the other side, when you'll know you persisted despite discomfort. You've got this.

☐ GET BETTER AT DIGGING DEEP

Challenges are part of life. They're not here to torture you or dictate your fate. They're here to help you grow. The next time you encounter a speed bump, view it as an opportunity to dig a little deeper and uncover a resilience that perhaps you didn't know you had. We've all got reserves that we generally don't think too much about—consider this your chance to rediscover what you're made of.

☐ GET OUT OF OVERWHELM

Overwhelm, worry, doubt—they're all different flavors of the same basic fear: that you don't have what it takes. But if the thing that's making you feel overwhelmed is something that you truly want, you absolutely do have what it takes—because where there's a want, there's a way. It only takes two steps to get out of overwhelm. Tell yourself *I've got this* and then take the next good step. These two things are all you ever need to do to stay on track.

☐ GIVE YOURSELF MORE CARROTS

Most of us were taught to use more sticks than carrots when pushing ourselves to get work done, but the threat of punishment is more about forcing compliance than inspiring great work. How can you use the stick less often on yourself and give yourself more carrots? It may be as simple as a change in thinking: *If I finish this by the end of the day, I'll join my friends for a glass of wine* rather than *If I don't finish by the end of the day, I can't go out tonight.* Or you may actually give yourself a reward—a pedicure, or an iced coffee (or green juice)—for raking the leaves or going through the stack of paperwork that has accumulated on your dining table. When you are more giving *to* yourself, you can ask more *of* yourself.

☐ TEND TO THE THING YOU CAN'T STOP THINKING ABOUT

That little voice that keeps telling you to take care of that one thing knows what it's talking about—whatever it is may seem like a minor detail, but all those little reminders imply that it's something worthy of your attention. What's been floating around in the back of your mind that you know needs your attention? Take care of it now if you can, and if you can't, set a reminder in your calendar for when you will.

☐ HARNESS THE POWER OF COMPOUND INTEREST

Compound interest—the financial phenomenon that happens when the interest you've earned on your initial investment starts earning interest, increasing your returns exponentially over time—has been described as the eighth wonder of the world. It applies to forming new habits too. Whatever positive habit you're thinking of adopting, start it now. A year from now, you'll be so glad you didn't let another year go by because the longer you do something over time, the more benefits it reaps.

TEND TO WHERE YOU ARE

Before you go making a bunch of new promises to yourself or to other people, examine the promises you've already made. Maybe you want to commit to working on your temper, but have you followed through on your promise to be a better listener? Before you promise the kids a trip to the resort, ask yourself what other promises you've made to them. Are you honoring those? If you're not, how can you? Taking great care of your existing responsibilities is the best and only way to naturally grow to the next level.

BE A LITTLE BIT LESS LAZY

Home makeover shows where an entire house gets transformed in under thirty minutes are popular for a reason—the idea of an instant overhaul is fantastically exciting. But let's face it: most of the time, setting a goal for sudden radical transformation is unrealistic and a setup for disappointment. Instead of aiming to be a whirling dervish of change, aim to simply be a little less lazy—start with the clean bathroom, work up to the immaculate home. It's much easier, and more productive over the long-term, than trying to reinvent yourself as a dynamo.

☐ PLAY TENNIS WITH SOMEONE A LITTLE BETTER THAN YOU

There's a well-known sports axiom that says that when you play tennis with someone who's better than you, you play better than you normally do. It applies to the rest of life too. Find a mastermind group, mentor, or an accountability partner who intimidates you a little bit—that's how you challenge yourself to get out of your comfort zone and improve your game.

☐ TAKE THE STAIRS

Personal development isn't an elevator, where you get in on the ground floor, quickly whoosh to the top, and stay there forever and ever. It's a staircase—each new level you attain brings the next level into view. And the staircase never ends, which may sound exhausting, but it means that there is always more insight, freedom, and gratification available. Always. Which is a wonderful thing.

PLAY THE LONG GAME

You can look for quick ways to make progress, but always keep in the back of your mind that you're playing a long game—if quick is your sole measurement of success, you'll feel like a failure even though you're making great progress over the long term. The next two, five, and ten years will pass whether or not you're working toward your goals—be the person who can look back and be thankful you kept going.

REFLECT ON YOUR PURPOSE

What do you believe you were put on this earth to do? If part of your mission is to help other people get out of debt as you once did, for example, that can not only inform your career path (you'd make a great personal finance writer, investment advisor, or money coach) but also help you make choices in your personal life. Thinking about what your purpose is will give you another touchstone to help you make decisions big and small and help you stay committed to fulfilling that purpose.

GET OUT OF THE HOUSE

Let's face it, it's rare for opportunity to seek you out where you live. Actually leaving the house makes it much more likely you'll have that chance run-in that leads to something great. To invite more fortuitous encounters into your life, say yes to more invitations, sign up for conferences, show up at lectures, and at least once a year get your butt on a plane, train, boat, or bus to connect with people or places that inspire you.

MAKE A REGULAR DATE WITH YOUR DREAMS

Looking back at how far you've come and charting where you want to go next keeps you present with your goals and your dreams. To make this part of your regular routine, take thirty minutes at the beginning of each month to review the month before and plan the one ahead. And at least once a year—around New Year's if that suits you, but it could be any time—take a whole day to look back, reflect, assess, and plan.

☐ GET A BUDDY

Of course it's good to be internally motivated, but having the accountability and support of a friend or two who are committed to a similar goal helps all of you stay on track. Start a neighborhood meditation group, get a walking buddy, or find an entrepreneurial friend to engage in fifteen-minute check-ins once a week to set weekly goals and report on last week's progress. Camaraderie is a powerful force—so make sure you choose a buddy who's dedicated to moving forward instead of one who'll pull you off track.

☐ WHEN YOU CAN'T DO A LOT, DO A LITTLE

Life will get busy and you will struggle to keep doing the things you want to do—this is not in question. In those instances, even the bare minimum counts. Taking a walk around the block at lunch when you don't have time for a longer excursion, for instance, will keep your seat warm and prevent you from feeling like you've completely fallen off the wagon. Forgiving yourself for your lapses also makes it that much easier to climb back up on the wagon when you get more of your time back.

KEEP YOUR EYES ON THE PRIZE

Any time you're trying to talk yourself out of doing something that you know is good for you, think about how good you'll feel after you've done it. This sounds overly simplistic, but you will want to focus instead on all the reasons why you don't want to do it. Anticipating your sense of accomplishment pulls you forward and out of the mud of resistance that's trying to pull you down.

GET HIP TO YOUR TRICKS

Most people are pretty good at pulling themselves off course when they're tired, discouraged, or just want a break already. Raising your awareness about the ways you try to derail yourself will help you not fall pray to them. Do you tell yourself that change is too hard? Or that you don't have the time? Or that you don't know what you're doing? The sooner you can recognize those same old tricks, the sooner you can keep moving despite them.

THINK ABOUT THE RIPPLES

In those inevitable moments where you're thinking about quitting, find inspiration in all the other lives you're touching. It may not be obvious at first, but challenge yourself to think about everyone involved: if you're adopting a healthier diet, your family, friends, and coworkers may get inspired by your example. If some of them decide to change their diets too, their friends, families, and coworkers will benefit. Your efforts spin a web of inspiration that can help you to keep going.

TIE THE THINGS YOU WANT TO DO TO THE THINGS YOU ALREADY DO

If you're looking for the time to add something new to your schedule, you might give up before you begin. Instead, think about what you're already doing and see where you can weave in something new. For example, you can practice mindfulness in the shower, listen to language instruction audios on your nightly dog walk, or keep your vitamins next to the coffee mugs. Adding something new to an already established part of your routine makes it relatively painless and doesn't require finding any additional time.

AUTOMATE WHAT YOU CAN

Staying committed doesn't always have to require effort. One of the blessings of our moment in history is the quantity and diversity of technological help at our disposal. Is there some way to automate progress toward your goal? For example, can you set up a recurring withdrawal from your checking account to go directly into savings? Or use an app to help you meditate? Use tools to make taking action easier.

BURN THE SHIPS

Worried the going might be too tough in the new world you're creating for yourself by acting on the advice in this book? Once you set foot in that new life, do as the explorer Cortés did and burn your ships. If there's something you want but haven't been able to grasp, and the outcome is critical to your well-being, consider making a no-going-back decision. For example, if you want to move to a new house that's better suited to your life and budget, give notice on your lease or put your current house on the market. There are times in everyone's life when the best way to move forward is to remove the option of staying put or retreating.

SET YOURSELF UP FOR SUCCESS

Starting something new generally requires less "stuff" than you might think. Still, sometimes acquiring a new item can really set you up for success: a good rain jacket makes a daily walking practice much more likely, just as new workout clothes makes going to the gym more enticing. The key is to start small. Invest in one thing that will ease your entry and buy other things you might need later—they can also be used as a reward for making progress.

QUIT IN A QUIET MOMENT

It's a human response to think about quitting when things get hard, but that's actually a terrible time to decide to bail. Why? Because moments of difficulty are painful, and when you're in pain you aren't thinking clearly. A better time to consider quitting is when things are quiet. Perhaps they're quiet because the goal you've set doesn't suit you. Maybe quitting that thing would free you up to go after something that's a better fit. And if the storm you're battling is one squall too many, tell yourself you'll move on as soon as it passes.

DO IT FOR YOURSELF

If you're trying to change for someone else, here's a truth for you: you have no control over what other people think of you. You may knock yourself out to impress them (whether you get the haircut, lose the weight, or get the tattoo), and they may not care, or even notice. So get clear on what it will mean to *you* to make the changes you're dreaming of. By taking steps to be a better version of yourself, you will naturally change how other people see you.

FORGET ABOUT THE MAP

You may love the idea of mapping out each step you'll take on the path to achieving your goal before you get started. But each step you take will give you feedback that will likely pull you off that carefully constructed course. Meaning, you don't really need it. All you ever need to do is take the next right step and trust that when you do, the step after that will make itself known.

BE STUBBORN ABOUT YOUR ENDS BUT FLEXIBLE ABOUT YOUR MEANS

When you let go of the idea of mapping out your every step, there is one thing you have to stay clear on—your end destination. You can be as stubborn as you want to be about where you're trying to get—a certain amount of debt paid off, a romantic relationship where you feel adored, a particular project that you want to launch. But being malleable about how you get there will help you navigate the inevitable twists and turns along the way. Once you get where you're going, it won't matter how you got there—it will only matter that you did.

INVITE OTHERS ALONG

To make your self-bettering efforts more communal and convivial, ask people you trust if they'd like to join you, whether as an official accountability partner or just as a companion. Having someone by your side as you go through the process can make it more rewarding and inspire you to reach a little further. Some people will have absolutely no interest in joining you, and that's okay. The right people will respond positively—they're the ones who'll either join you or sincerely root you on.

SHARE WISELY, AND WITH AN ENTHUSIASTIC EAR

We all have people in our lives who are prone to worry or tend to be cautious—these are not the folks you want to confide in about your efforts to be a better person. Because despite their good intentions, they're likely to say something that plants a seed of doubt in your mind. Think about who's most likely to be supportive and enthusiastic on your behalf—that's who you want to share your intentions with.

UP THE FUN FACTOR

Being committed doesn't have to mean all work and no play. When you set out to work on anything that will help you be a better person, do something to make the experience fun—play some music, wear something you love, light a delicious-smelling candle, pour yourself a glass of wine, or make a perfect cup of coffee. It's completely okay to appeal to your inner hedonist in these moments, because when we enjoy our efforts, we look forward to them and want to get started again.

PART SEVEN

Work Well

Being a better person means doing
the right thing in all parts of your life—
including when you're on the clock. By upping
your game at work, you have a chance to not
only do well for yourself but to elevate your
company's impact, which can help you positively affect a lot of other people's lives too,
including those of your coworkers and the
clients you ultimately serve.

The tools in this chapter will help
you focus more, get more done, be a better
coworker, grow your skill set, and give yourself
the balance you need to stay energized
and fulfilled.

☐ MONO-TASK ONE THING A DAY

Multitasking is a fact of life and can sometimes be useful, but it's not always the best choice. When you work on the most important thing on your daily to-do list, invite your best thinking by closing your email program, putting your phone on airplane mode, blocking yourself from social media, and doing one thing. You'll get it done more effectively and efficiently when you do.

☐ DISCOVER YOUR SUPERPOWERS

It's easy to dismiss the things that come naturally to you, because we tend to undervalue things that don't feel like "hard work," but these things you do easily are your superpowers. They help you make a bigger impact with less exertion. To discover your talents, ask yourself, *What do people compliment me on? What do I do without even thinking? Where do I do my best meddling?* Naming these talents will help you own them and put them to good use.

☐ PUT YOUR SUPERPOWERS TO GOOD USE

Okay, you know what your innate talents are. Now your work is to find more opportunities to use them. If you're a natural questioner, seek ways to do more research in your work. If you're great at making people feel comfortable, consider a move into client relations. You may not be able to customize a position that uses every one of your talents, but when you lean into your strengths you'll naturally start on a trajectory that suits you.

SHARE THE STAGE

Authors are lucky—they get an acknowledgments page to call out everyone who helped them write the book, directly or indirectly. You may not have a similar avenue in which to share your thanks, but find a way to do it anyway. Send out a team email thanking everyone who helped you achieve a goal at work, give a toast at a celebratory dinner acknowledging the people who helped you reach that milestone, tell a story at your next meeting about the ways your colleagues contributed to a recent achievement. As anyone who's taken an improv class can tell you, it takes presence, courage, and trust to share the stage with other people—all traits that will help draw quality people and opportunities to you.

MAKE A LEARNING PLAN

If you want your career to continue to grow, you need your skills and interests to keep evolving too. Ensure your growth by making a plan to keep learning. What skill would really serve you at work? Or, what have you always wanted to do but don't know how? Just like you want to dress for the job you want, not the one you have, you also want to learn things that will help you do the job you aspire to.

PICK YOURSELF

We spend a lot of time waiting to be picked—for the job, the promotion, the cool project. Wanting to be recognized by the powers that be is such a normal part of life that you've likely lost touch with how often you do it and how disempowering it is. If there's a project you want to work on, tell your boss you want in (and explain why you're a good fit and how you'll balance it with your other responsibilities). If there's a different job you'd like to transfer into, take a class to build the skills you'd need in that role. Whatever you do, don't just wait for it to happen. When you start to create your own opportunities instead of waiting for them to come along, you empower yourself. And that's when things start changing for the better.

TRY LESS HARD, GET MORE DONE

Free up time and energy by identifying the parts of your job that don't have a lot of impact—things like triple-checking your work, putting in face time, or gossiping—and then choose to care a little less about them. A good way to enforce that choice is to put more time and energy into the important things—which are things that deliver value to either the bottom line or your end client (ideally, both). Doing so will naturally crowd out any overwork you might be doing on the stuff that just doesn't matter.

☐ SIT IN THE FRONT OF THE ROOM

You walk into a large meeting room set up with rows of chairs. Where do you sit? Do you slink into a seat in the back? Or into an aisle seat so you can make a quick getaway? Where you sit reveals a lot about your approach to life. Try heading straight for the front of the room. Build your tolerance for taking up prime real estate and for being that visible. It's a little thing that signifies something big—that you're okay with being seen and that you're moving toward life, not away from it.

☐ BE COACHABLE

Everyone has a blind spot or two—a weakness that they can't perceive. There's no shame in it. So when someone you trust points out a habit or a pattern that appears to be holding you back, be receptive to what he has to say and game for trying a different approach. In other words, be coachable. This is someone you trust, after all. Resisting objective feedback is a sure way to stay stuck.

☐ TEND TO YOUR NETWORK

Your extended network of friends, colleagues, class-mates, and acquaintances is a crucial ingredient of your career success. You can't keep in touch with everyone all the time, but you can keep connections strong with just a little thoughtful effort—decide the handful of people you'll connect with monthly, the dozen or so folks you'll check in with seasonally, and the rest you'll contact yearly. Now put reminders in your calendar to match. Reaching out to ask how they are—with a small update of your own—is all it takes.

☐ TALK TO YOUR COLLEAGUE BEFORE YOU TALK TO HER BOSS

If you're having an issue with someone you work with, speak with her directly about it before you go to her boss. It's professional courtesy, and it's also your responsibility to try to improve a situation before you involve a third party. This gives the coworker in question a chance to course-correct before she attracts what might be negative attention too.

GIVE BETTER FEEDBACK

If you have to give a direct report constructive criticism, set an intention to be curious (instead of judgmental) and helping her grow (instead of reprimanding) before you call her into your office. If your report has been missing deadlines, for example, she may have something going on in her personal life that you don't know about, and merely giving her a warning won't help the situation. Establish trust first by saying something like, "I'm guessing you're feeling a little nervous, scared, or angry right now. Are any of those true?" Once you've had some sincere dialogue, explain why you called her in, share what you've noticed, and ask for her thoughts on how to address it—then work out a strategy together. It's important to manage your own emotions about the situation first. If you call her into your office when you're angry, odds are good you won't be able to listen and she'll get defensive, leaving you both upset. You want to be able to keep a light tone and positive (or at least neutral) facial expressions—otherwise your message won't penetrate and you'll miss an opportunity for both of you to grow.

ASK DUMB QUESTIONS

If you're confused about something, chances are someone else is too. So don't be afraid to raise your hand and ask for more information. The person you're asking will benefit too, because it's always clarifying to try and explain something more simply. (The one exception, of course, is asking a question because you were late or simply weren't paying attention—in that case, ask someone else who was there to catch you up afterward.)

BUILD A BUFFER

The idea that you can manage time—which is, after all, a natural force subject to its own laws—is misleading. Really, all you can manage are your expectations. So here's a way to give yourself the experience of having more time: start overestimating how long things will take. Block out forty-five minutes for what should be a thirty-minute meeting. If you think you can write a presentation in two hours, give yourself three. It will protect you from constantly feeling rushed as one meeting bleeds in to the other or successive tasks take longer than you expect. When you stop rushing, you're able to be more present—and a little less annoyed in general.

☐ CHECK EMAIL LESS

Research has found that checking email less—three times a day, to be exact—provided as much of a reduction in stress levels as practicing relaxation techniques. It also saves time—you still send as many emails but spend 20 percent less time doing it. Use an app (such as SelfControl) to hold you accountable and set specific times of day when you won't check in, and when you will—and make sure it's never just before bed.

☐ REWORK BAD IDEAS INSTEAD OF DISMISSING THEM

An idea that's proven itself unworkable is worthless—right? Well, not necessarily. So-called "bad" ideas often have the seed of a great idea in them, because ideas rarely emerge fully formed. (A classic example is *YouTube,* which started as a video dating site.) Many times it's the quarter-turn that makes everything align, not the 180-degree shift.

☐ DELEGATE BETTER

Is it really worth it to ask someone else to take some nonvital tasks off your plate? It is if you do it well. (If you delegate and then micromanage, everyone would prefer you just did it yourself.) Give instructions to ask for help if the person gets stuck, but otherwise, let them at it. People who are doing something for the first time may make mistakes—focus on appreciating the effort more than the results at first and give positive feedback they can hear.

☐ TAKE ON UNCOMFORTABLE TASKS

If you stick to tasks that you already know you can do well, you won't develop at work. Find manageable ways to try new things. For example, if you want to establish more of a voice in meetings with higher-ups, start speaking up more in meetings of your peers. Accept your missteps and view them as ways to refine your skills. Growth can be uncomfortable, but so is staying in the same place for too long.

☐ DECLARE AN END TO THE WORKDAY

Fred Flintstone knew when the whistle blew that work was done. Many of us don't have those same kind of delineators in this age of twenty-four-seven connectivity, but it doesn't mean you don't need one. Even if your job demands connectedness, try to set your own rules for when you officially end your workday. Your boss or a client may text you at odd hours, but you don't have to be the one starting the conversations. The boundaries you set protect you from overload and burnout—and that's in everyone's best interest.

☐ MAKE A BETTER TRANSITION BETWEEN WORK AND PERSONAL LIFE

In addition to declaring an end to your workday, help yourself transition back into civilian mode by creating a simple ritual that helps you leave work stress at work—take the scenic way home from work, hit the gym, go on a walk, sing your brains out on the drive home, meditate for five minutes before you get out of the car. If you're bringing your work mindset into your personal time, you're short-changing yourself.

TAKE TIME OFF

In the average year, Americans let 658 million paid vacation days go unused. Repeat: 658 million days of paid vacation time, wasted! Now consider that family trips are one of the things kids remember most about childhood. Whether or not you have kids, take your vacation. Your life, your relationships, and even your bank account will be richer for it. Research has found that people who take their vacation days are more likely to get a raise or a bonus, not less.

SET BETTER DAILY GOALS

If your to-do list includes every single thing you ever need to get done, it will still be miles long at the end of the day despite how hard you work. That's a recipe for frustration. Instead, keep a master list of everything in a different spot than your calendar or planner. Each morning, choose a handful of those items to put on your daily to-do list. Maintaining these two lists will help you feel good about your progress without worrying that you're forgetting something.

☐ PRIORITIZE FIRST

This may take all the willpower you've got, but it is so worth it: make the first thing you do every morning be setting your priorities for the day—and *not* checking your messages. If you wait until after you've gone through your inbox to prioritize, you'll start the day in reactive instead of proactive mode. Your thinking is clearest first thing in the morning; put that clarity to good use instead of frittering it away on emails.

☐ GET BETTER AT PRIORITIZING

Here are some guidelines for setting priorities in a way that helps you focus on the important instead of merely the urgent: Think about the things on your list that make the biggest impact *and* that mean the most to you—those are your highest priorities. Next come the things that have a big impact, even though you may not love them. For things that don't move the needle and that you don't enjoy, either delegate them or bang them out in one concentrated burst.

SHINE BRIGHTER

Someone will always be more experienced or skilled at work than you. But there's one area where you can choose to shine, every time, and that's in your mind-set. It may seem a bit frivolous at first glance, but ask any chief executive, small-business owner, or other leader: every organization—even one-woman shops—needs people with heart, positivity, and gumption. You don't need any additional training or responsibility to be one of those people. You can decide to show up that way starting today. Do so by asking yourself, *Where can I make an impact today*? Whether it's something concrete, like volunteering for a task, or something softer, like a well-timed word of encouragement, know that even small efforts can create a big boost in morale for you and your colleagues.

DON'T PASS ON BAD TREATMENT

If someone yells at you at work, resist the urge to bring that upset home and yell at the kids, pick a fight with your spouse, or be mean to the dog. Find ways to let your anger out before you get home. A vigorous walk around the block, a kickboxing class, an angry letter that you never—never—send can all take the edge off so you can start fresh when you get home.

◼ MANAGE YOUR MOOD AT WORK

A lot happens in a typical workday, and much of it we have no control over—the snippy email, the unpleasant task that landed on your desk. Resist the urge to distract yourself with gossip or complaining. Remember: a shared workplace isn't an appropriate venue for the display of many natural human moods, and coworkers expect to be treated with respect and professionalism. Ask a coworker to tell you something good that happened or make your own list of things that have gone right that day, no matter how small. The things you place your focus on take on a bigger presence in your mind, and choosing to focus on the good will also lift your mood.

◼ FOCUS ON DELIVERING VALUE

Wanting to do a good job is honorable, but it can also be paralyzing, in part because the definition of "good" is subjective and your inner critic may equate it with "perfect." To get you moving on daunting tasks, think about the value you'll be delivering. How do your end clients stand to benefit from your efforts? Will they get more profits, more support, more peace of mind? Knowing the final result you're trying to create will help motivate you to get going, and keep going.

☐ GO FOR THE LOW-HANGING FRUIT

Big projects can be so overwhelming that you do nothing. The secret to getting out of overwhelm is to remember that you only ever need to determine the next right step. And then take it. Taking some small action—particularly one that's easy—will help you start building momentum. After that, you'll be too busy to doubt yourself.

☐ SEEK OUT A MENTOR

Mentors provide invaluable insight and support that help you elevate your career faster and more efficiently than you can on your own. So as you tend to your network, keep an eye out for someone who might able to play that role for you. If you can't find a mentor, hire a coach—look for someone who has expertise in the area where you'd like support, and with whom you also feel a good personal connection. Coaches in general can get a bad rap, but there wouldn't be so many of them if they weren't fulfilling a need. Put an encouraging voice in your ear to keep you on track.

BECOME A BETTER WRITER

Your work may have nothing to do with writing, per se, but how you string words together in emails, reports, and presentations plays a big role in how effective you are and the impression you make. Ask a friend with a flare for writing to edit a few of your pieces, highlighting their changes, so you can see what needs tightening up. No one like that comes immediately to mind? Here's an easy and effective tip: whenever you can, write a first draft, set it aside for a day, and then look at it with fresh eyes. You'll be able to quickly identify and address mistakes before sending it out.

IF YOU'RE NOT THE RIGHT PERSON, REFER

When you're asked to pitch in on something that you know isn't for you—not your business, not your skill set, not your interest—suggest a person or other resource that you think would be a better fit. This isn't about passing the buck; it's about helping the asker find what he needs and passing along an opportunity to someone who has the potential to appreciate it.

SAY THE RIGHT THING AFTER "I DON'T KNOW"

Nobody enjoys looking stupid, but no one has all the answers either. At some point, you're going to be asked something you don't know the answer to. Rather than being mortified, or bluffing, all you have to do is admit you don't know the answer and then commit to finding it out. Throwing in a "That's a great question" or "I wonder who we could check in with on this" shows that you're open to identifying the holes in your knowledge.

GET AHEAD BY BEING WHERE YOU ARE

If you were an employer, who would you want to promote? The person who is dotting every *i* in her current position? Or the person who is slacking because she's gunning for a promotion? Any time you want to move up to the next level, take impeccable care of your existing deliverables. It shows you are the kind of person who takes on and embraces responsibility, which always makes a favorable impression.

☐ NEGOTIATE BETTER

Negotiation is a collaboration, not a battle. Getting better at it is empowering and helps you get what you want. Here are some basic principles to make it less fraught: Seek to understand what the other party wants. Be creative in thinking up ways to meet those wants as well as your own. Listen more than you talk. If you accept less—a lower salary for example—ask for something in return—more time off, a more flexible schedule, etc. Finally, get comfortable with being quiet and waiting for a response. A successful negotiation is one that satisfies both parties—be patient, get creative, and get there!

☐ FINISH STRONG

Athletes know that victory is often decided in the last few moments of a contest—the chest-thrust of a sprinter or the outstretched fingers of a swimmer mean the difference between gold and silver. While your work project likely isn't as once-in-a-lifetime as an Olympic event, learning to manage your energy so that you have some gas in the tank for the end stages will improve your results exponentially with only incrementally greater effort.

■ WORK SMARTER, NOT HARDER

The eighty/twenty rule—otherwise known as the Pareto principle for the late nineteenth-century economist Vilfredo Pareto who noticed that 80 percent of the land in Italy was owned by 20 percent of the people—says that 80 percent of your results comes from 20 percent of your efforts. Spend some time thinking about the simple actions that, when done consistently, result in big strides toward your goals—strengthening relationships with the 20 percent of your clients who generate 80 percent of revenue, for example, or making sure you get ninety minutes (approximately 20 percent of an eight-hour day) of focused time to produce your best work (no meetings or *Facebook*ing allowed). Now make sure you prioritize those needle movers when planning what you'll get done in a day or a week. Small, meaningful steps taken with consistency can take you everywhere you want to go.

■ SET GOALS THAT STRETCH YOU

If you only ever set goals that you know you can hit, you may never get out of your comfort zone, which is where the magic happens. Let's say you set ten quarterly goals: make one of them something that feels at least mildly impossible. "This might be crazy, but I would love to _____." Make it related to something that excites you, and give yourself permission to surprise yourself. Going after a big goal will stretch you. It will also make you stronger.

☐ DEVELOP YOUR ABILITY TO FOCUS

The ability to focus seems a rarer commodity every year—the (potentially) good news is that as such, it's getting more and more valuable. Take stock of what you already know about creating the conditions for focused work, and educate yourself about some new techniques that help you get in the zone and do great work. Honing your ability to pay attention will help you stand out, make you feel less scattered, and serve you well in all your pursuits, at work and in the rest of your life.

☐ REDEFINE WINNING

There are many ways to think about "winning." It could mean that you've defeated someone else. Or it could mean that you've hit a personal milestone, or succeeded alongside a team. How do you define it? As motivating as it might be to want to crush your competition, you'll probably get a lot more gratification out of outperforming your previous efforts or succeeding with others than you will from vanquishing rivals.

☐ WELCOME QUESTIONS

When presenting your thoughts, whether in a formal presentation or in a team meeting, be sure to save time for questions. It's not the equivalent of a pop quiz that you could potentially fail, it's a chance to customize your thoughts to specific situations, which ultimately helps clarify your thinking. If someone asks a question you don't know the answer to, all you have to do is say, "I don't know the answer to that. I'll have to look into it further and get back to you." And then be sure to do so.

☐ THINK ABOUT HOW YOU PRESENT YOURSELF

Whether you think about it or not, the clothes you wear to work send a message about who you are and how you want to be seen. What do you want that message to be? Do you want to be seen as a trend-setter or buttoned-up? Do you want to blend in to the background or stand out? You don't need to be obsessed with your appearance, but do be thoughtful about what you're trying to convey.

☐ EMBRACE THE THREE STAGES OF WORK

Anyone who's ever worked in a restaurant can tell you that there are three distinct phases to cooking—prepping, the actual cooking, and cleanup. These three phases apply to any project. If you're planning an event, for example, there's the work required before the event, during the event itself, and then not only dismantling the space but also doing a postmortem so that you know what you can improve on next time. Being mindful of each phase and allotting time for each one boosts effectiveness and serenity, as knowing where you are in the process provides a certain level of peace.

☐ GET MORE SKILLFUL AT IDENTIFYING PROBLEMS

Albert Einstein said, "If I had an hour to solve a problem, I would spend fifty-five minutes thinking about the problem and five minutes thinking about the solution." Einstein was noting that the problem has its solution buried within it. When you're faced with solving a problem at work, first put on your detective's hat and investigate the true nature of the problem. Does that other department have a personnel problem, or could this be a communication issue? Should you post a sign reminding people to shut the door completely, or should you replace the balky latch? When you consider a problem from many angles, your solution is much more likely to address the root rather than merely the symptom.

PLAN YOUR LEISURE TIME

The thought of planning your time off may seem like an oxymoron—if it does, you may not be making the most of your personal time. Don't leave your recharge and recovery time entirely to chance—you and your loved ones want to enjoy it as best you can. Spending some time midweek thinking about what you want to do this weekend makes it much more likely that you will actually do those things. Don't worry, you don't have to plan every moment. You just have to give some thought to what you want to do and when you'll do it.

BOOK YOUR WORK TIME

Focusing on important work requires good chunks of time, which won't magically appear on your calendar if you don't schedule them. Each week, look at your schedule and decide beforehand when you'll be at your desk, working on producing your deliverables rather than, for example, attending meetings. Then schedule those blocks of time in your calendar and don't accept meeting requests or schedule phone calls in those hours.

☐ MAKE TIME FOR YOUR SOUL WORK

Every job comes with a long list of responsibilities, but you have an obligation to do the work that speaks to your soul too, even if it doesn't show up anywhere on that list. When you plan your week, make sure to block out a chunk or two of time that you can devote to the work that's speculative—the proposal for the new project, or even the art you create on the side that keeps you a passionate and engaged person—because that energy will spill over into the narrower confines of your "job" too.

☐ TELL HER ABOUT THE SPINACH

Your after-lunch meeting is about to start when you notice a coworker has spinach in her teeth. Sure, it's awkward, but it would be much worse for her to realize after the meeting that it's been there all along. Tell her about the situation with as much clarity and lightness as you can, because surreptitiously gesturing toward her mouth will only make her confused. Stay with her long enough to let her know when it's completely gone.

☐ REACH OUT TO THE NEW PERSON

Starting a new job is equal parts exciting and scary. You don't have to be best friends with every new teammate, but you can certainly be part of the group that makes her feel welcome. A great way to make a new hire feel at home is to give her a piece of paper with your email address on it, and say, "In case you have any questions you're too embarrassed to ask out loud."

☐ MAKE A NEW POT OF COFFEE

Every pot of coffee will eventually meet its end. Many people will take that last cup and put the empty carafe back on the burner—*not my problem*! Be the person who takes the minute or so it requires to make a new pot, if for no other reason than because you'd hope someone would do the same for you. And hey—if it's the second-to-last cup, that legitimately isn't your problem!

DO YOUR DISHES

If it's tempting to dump your empty takeout containers in the office sink so you can get back to work more quickly: resist that temptation. People really, really don't like this! Unless there is someone who is being paid to keep the kitchen clean, your dishes are your responsibility—think of it as the metaphorical equivalent of picking up your dog's poop. It's just the right thing to do. (Also: if the food in the fridge doesn't belong to you, eating it *isn't* your responsibility.)

REMEMBER THE MISSION

When work gets hard, go back and reread the mission statement of the company. (If you work for yourself and you don't have a mission statement, write one.) Remembering the goals that the company is aiming to achieve can reinspire you and help you take a bigger-picture perspective to whatever obstacle may be in your path.

PART EIGHT

Let Go of Your Stuff

While you don't have to become
a full-on minimalist in order to be a better
person, acquiring and tending to possessions
definitely eats up a lot of time, space, money,
and energy. And those are precious resources
that could be put to use on more productive
things, like developing relationships, deepen-
ing your skills, giving back, and having
meaningful experiences.

In this chapter, you'll learn
strategies to help you buy a little less, take
better care of what you've got, and get rid of
what doesn't serve you. It's all in the name
of lightening your load and freeing you up
to pursue better things.

☐ GET ELECTRICITY-SMART

Challenge yourself to use electricity more mindfully—turn off lights when you leave a room, unplug appliances you aren't using and any fully charged devices, and install a programmable thermostat to turn down the heat when you're not home. Your bills will be lower and so will your carbon footprint.

☐ WEAN FROM THE SCREEN

Smartphones are amazing tools, but overusing them can degrade your posture, your tolerance for downtime, and your ability to connect with yourself and with others. Reduce habitual use by making some parts of your life screen-free, whether it's a physical area like the dinner table, a regular event—your morning walk is a great time to leave the phone in your pocket—or a time of day, say after nine p.m. With practice, you can curb your habit of reaching for it every time you have ten seconds to yourself.

☐ TURN OFF THE WI-FI EACH NIGHT

Wean from the screen *and* reduce your electricity use by using a timer to switch off your Wi-Fi router each night (say at eleven p.m.) and automatically start it up again the next morning. You'll likely sleep better too, because you won't be tempted to stream another episode, you'll reduce your exposure to the stimulating light your devices emit, and there will be one less source of electromagnetic fields (EMFs) in your home, which have been shown to impact sleep cycles.

☐ LEARN THE FINE ART OF FIXING THINGS

Your grandmother knew how to do all kinds of basic repair—get a stain out, sew a button, patch a torn knee, and darn a sock. You may not have received that training, but *YouTube* makes it easy to teach yourself. There's something incredibly gratifying about restoring a damaged but otherwise perfectly good item to a usable state. You'll also be teaching your kids to be fixers and makers, and less-than-automatic consumers.

REPAIR BEFORE YOU REPLACE

There will be some things you can't repair on your own, but a professional may be able to get the job done. Can you reupholster your couch instead of buying a new one? Fix the fridge? Get a new zipper for your favorite pair of pants? This helps create the habit of using your existing resources before acquiring more. If the repair isn't cost-effective, by all means, replace. At least you'll know you tried to save something from the landfill.

CONSIDER "NO GIFT" BIRTHDAY PARTIES

For kids or for grownups, consider adopting a "no gifts" policy for birthday parties. Having a party where the only expectation is the celebration helps teach kids to value people and moments, instead of things. (Children can get gifts from their closest friends and loved ones separately.) Another option is to ask for people to give a card with $5 to save up for one bigger, more special present, which introduces the concept of saving.

SET UP YOUR SPACE
FOR RELAXATION

Getting out a few things that help you relax and putting them where you will see them makes it way more likely that you'll actually use them. Set up your yoga mat in a corner of your bedroom, create some clear table space to leave out a jigsaw puzzle, clean off the chair in your room that typically holds dirty clothes and put a great book next to it. Even when you aren't using those spaces, looking at them will help you remember the good feelings you've generated there.

MAKE YOUR CAR A
TRANQUIL SPACE

Make your car a rolling chamber of serenity by removing all trash every time you exit and enter and adding in a few key things that help you relax, such as a pretty rock to keep in your console, a picture of someone you love tucked in to the visor, and perhaps some orange peels and cloves in the ashtray to give off a soothing scent.

PUT THOSE DUSTY DUMBBELLS TO GOOD USE

You've likely got exercise equipment tucked in a closet somewhere. Make space to keep it out and you'll be much more likely to use it. Clear a floor space big enough for a yoga mat so you can stretch or do push-ups, hang the pull-up bar in a doorway and hang from it whenever you walk through, and keep the hand weights in your bedroom so you can lift weights before you get dressed. It all counts.

BUY LOCAL

When you do buy new things, buying from local stores—even if it's a chain store located in your town—instead of online saves the extra costs and pollution of shipping to your door, creates jobs for your neighbors, and generates tax revenues for your town. It also gives you an opportunity to see and chitchat with your neighbors, which is no small thing.

BUY ORGANIC

Chemicals, pesticides, and antibiotics used in the conventional food supply threaten your health when you consume that food, and also taint the environment through the soil and through runoff into the water supply. To advocate for a less chemical-laden world and to support farms that have less of a toxic footprint, spend the extra money to buy organic when you can.

WASTE LESS FOOD

According to the EPA, nearly 15 percent of all municipal trash is food that costs the average American family $1,600 each year. Reduce those amounts by buying only what you need, eating more leftovers, sharing entrées at restaurants, and composting. Most importantly, shop in your own refrigerator and pantry before you go to the store, and make a meal plan that uses what you have so you buy less in the first place.

GROW AT LEAST A TINY BIT OF YOUR OWN FOOD

You don't have to be a master gardener to experience the thrill of growing your own food: a big pot in a sunny spot can host a thriving tomato plant. A small plant on a well-lit windowsill can keep you with basil all summer long. You can even regrow much of the produce you buy at the grocery store—celery and green onions, for example, will regenerate after you cut them if you keep them in a cup of water.

USE YOUR OWN BAGS

The plastic used to make plastic bags takes somewhere between one hundred and four hundred years to decompose, and there are eighty-eight million tons of it produced every year. Using your own reusable bags is not only kinder to the environment, but it also gives you a chance to think about exactly how much stuff you're going to buy before you start shopping, which helps you self-regulate and ultimately generate less waste.

EMBRACE ORDER

The average person spends fifteen minutes a day looking for a lost item—that's a lot of unnecessary stress on a daily basis, and over the course of a year, that's more than ninety-one hours spent on panicked searching. Reclaim those hours by putting your keys, wallet, purse, and phone in the same spot every night. You'll also dramatically improve your baseline stress level, and especially on your way out the door in the morning. You know what it's like to have to leave in frustration wearing the wrong belt, or with the wrong shoes on. Spare yourself, and know where everything goes.

MAKE YOUR BED

Self-help gurus and military personnel agree—making your bed every morning is a recipe for starting the day off feeling accomplished, grown-up, in control, and happy. After all, your bed is your respite, and perhaps the only place you have that's dedicated to resting and recharging. That's a pretty important spot—you're in it for at least a quarter of your life—and it deserves the minute or two it takes to keep it tidy and welcoming.

ORGANIZE YOUR
DYSFUNCTIONAL SPACES

Think about a spot in your home that makes your life a little more difficult—the cluttered kitchen counter that makes it harder to cook, the stack of mail on the dining table that adds an aura of stress to your eating area, the overstuffed closet that makes getting dressed a minor ordeal. Choose one spot to make more functional (call in a friend or professional if you need help). The direct benefits are reward enough, and you'll also feel better every time you use that space.

LIBERATE WHAT YOU
ALREADY OWN

How many times have you bought baking soda or some other pantry staple that you already had because you couldn't find it in your cluttered cabinets? At least once a year, take the time to clear out and rearrange your drawers and shelves so that you don't have to keep rebuying what you can't find. If organizing really isn't your thing, this is a great task for a professional or a young relative looking to make some extra money.

☐ TAKE ONLY WHAT YOU NEED

Take one stroll down the cereal aisle and you'll know that we live in a world of excess, both in the sheer number of choices available to us and in the massive sizes those choices come in (a forty-eight-pack of toilet paper, anyone?). By taking only what you need for the immediate future, you send a signal that you trust that there will be more when you need more.

☐ SPEND MORE MONEY ON DOING THAN HAVING

Research has shown that the money you spend on experiences—trips, meals, events—elicits more feelings of gratitude than money that goes to purchasing more stuff—couches, handbags, clothes. And gratitude reduces stress and breeds feelings of connection and generosity. Saving up for a trip can also help dissuade you from buying things you don't truly need without feeling deprived.

WHEN YOU DO BUY THINGS, CHOOSE THINGS YOU CAN FEEL GOOD ABOUT

Whether you realize it or not, the things you spend your money on reflect your values. To be a more conscious consumer, maximize the money you spend on things you feel good about—the local business, the company that donates a portion of profits, the service that improves your life—and less on what doesn't—memberships you never use, clothes you rarely wear, gadgets you don't really need.

BE A BETTER MONEY STEWARD

If you'd like less money stress in your life, start by taking care of the money you have. Open and organize your bills, make a list of your outstanding debts, round up and use your gift cards, gather up your spare change and store it in a pretty cup or bowl. When you feel good about how you tend to your current money situation, you'll make decisions that perpetuate that feeling.

SEE HOW YOU SPEND

It's one thing to have a basic idea of where your money goes, but it's quite another to see the actual numbers. For at least one month (although more is better, some is better than none), make note of every dollar you spend and assign it a category. At the end of the month, tally up your category totals. Do it for the sake of gathering information instead of passing judgment, and for spending money more wisely going forward.

MODEL CONSUMING LESS TO YOUR KIDS

It's so tempting to meet your kid's every desire for something new. But getting accustomed to constantly getting new things can set the stage for a lifetime of mindless buying. Use a chore chart that needs to be filled up before making big purchases; give them a spending allowance so they can start learning how to balance their desires with their available funds; become regulars at the library. Because modeling is the most important way kids learn, let them hear you talk about how you decide what to buy and when. And then challenge yourself to make fewer impulse buys.

☐ SHOP FIRST IN YOUR OWN CLOSET

Whenever you start to get the itch to add to your wardrobe, get in the habit of looking in your closet and dresser drawers before you head to the store—it will help you see what you truly need before you wade into the sea of temptation of the stores. Also, you may discover that you already have something that works.

☐ SHOP CONSIGNMENT BEFORE HEADING TO THE MALL

Buying your clothes secondhand serves many important purposes—it reuses perfectly good items and helps reduce demand for new clothes to be made. You also stand to save a ton of money, as "used" clothes (many of which still have tags on them) cost a fraction of new clothes, making it feel like a treasure hunt instead of a splurge you'll pay for all over again later with a surge of guilt when the credit card bill comes due.

HOST A CLOTHING SWAP

Here's one more way to refresh your wardrobe without buying new—invite friends to come to your house and bring anything in their closet they're no longer wearing. Everyone gets to shop from everyone else's castoffs— you leave with new-to-you items, your unused clothes and shoes find a new home, and what doesn't get taken home can be donated. It's a fun night with low-stress and long-lasting benefits.

BORROW MORE THINGS

Talk to your neighbors about divvying up bigger purchases—you buy the snow blower, someone else has the lawnmower, and the house three doors down keeps the weed whacker and hedge trimmer. More and more libraries are starting to lend things besides just books, too, including tools, sports gear, digital equipment, and musical instruments. Sharing resources does more than save money; it also frees you from some of the spatial and psychic load that comes from being responsible for an ever-growing list of things.

HAVE A YARD SALE

A yard sale creates a lot of good. It gives you an excuse to weed out things you no longer need, puts a little extra money in your pocket, and gives you a great excuse to talk to your neighbors. Play some tunes, make a tasty beverage, and you've got yourself a fun Saturday morning too. Going in with another family or two or three only adds to the social element and makes it more likely that you'll draw a crowd.

USE UNWANTED STUFF TO RAISE FUNDS FOR CHARITY

Maybe the thought of having a yard sale sounds like too much work. No problem. Just round up all that stuff you're not using and either drop it off at your local thrift store or have them come pick it up (many will). Your unused and unwanted stuff will generate money for a great cause, you'll free up space in your life, and you'll have that Saturday morning that you would otherwise spend on a yard sale for other things.

DON'T KEEP GIFTS YOU DON'T LIKE

Yes, it really is okay to regift, and yes, even that sweater from Mom. Gifts have a strong sentimental pull, but if you truly don't like or use them, you aren't doing yourself or the gift-giver any favors by keeping them around. This is especially true if every time you look at or think about the gift you feel guilty. It truly is the thought that counts—not the thing itself. You don't need to break Mom's heart—just make it your mission to get those items to someone who appreciates them.

FIND NEW PURPOSES FOR OLD THINGS

Before you toss an item that doesn't appear to be usable anymore, ask if there's some other way you can use it. For example, a sock that lost its mate in the dryer makes a great glasses case; a stained sweater makes for a good layer to wear when doing yard work; a chipped plate can be broken up and used to create a drainage space at the bottom of a planter. If you're heading in the other direction and trying to purge, by all means toss or donate it—but if you're throwing out a ripped T-shirt but you have a car waiting to be washed...see how that works?

COMMEMORATE WHAT YOU DON'T KEEP

There are some items that are more difficult to purge than others, especially kids' art projects, things that belonged to someone who has passed on, or mementos from your own childhood. In these instances, taking a picture of the thing can make it easier to get rid of it—keep the memory, not the thing. By doing so, you'll create space for new memories to come into your life.

RETHINK STORAGE

It may seem practical to hold on to things you like but don't have a need for—so you won't have to go out and repurchase it later—but is it wise to spend money and space on keeping things you never use? After all, you have to pay to insure it, to control its climate, and rent the space, potentially for years... Challenge yourself to let go of things you aren't currently using. If you need one again at some point, that's what *Craigslist* is for.

THINK ABOUT WHO WILL BE CLEANING OUT YOUR HOUSE

This is admittedly morbid, but it's a fact of life nonetheless. At some point, someone you love will be charged with going through your possessions and deciding what to do with every single thing you own. Let this knowledge empower you to make more of the tough decisions about what to keep and what to let go of so they won't have to.

EXAMINE YOUR RECURRING MONTHLY PAYMENTS

Recurring payments are convenient, but how convenient is it to pay for something that you don't use? Not very. The next time you get your credit card bills, go through and look for the gym membership or online service you never use and take the fifteen minutes needed to cancel them. You'll plug up money leaks and create more room in your budget for things you actually want to do.

DEVELOP A SYSTEM FOR PAPERWORK

Here's a simple formula to contain the river of paperwork that flows through every household: get a desktop organizer for things that need attention in the next thirty days (bills, invitations, school notices), a filing cabinet for things you need semi-regular access to (receipts, tax returns, insurance documents), and a storage bin for things you need once in a blue moon (old tax returns, leases, wills).

REDUCE HOW MUCH MAIL YOU GET

Every four months, as many trees are cut down to make paper for junk mailings as are found in the Rocky Mountain National Forest. Save more trees—and save yourself the headache of going through piles of unwanted mail by unsubscribing from catalogs and direct mail. There are lots of apps and websites that can help with this project—OptOutPrescreen.com, CatalogChoice.org, and DMAchoice.org are a few—or you can search the web for ways to unsubscribe from and opt out from direct mailings.

ASSESS HOW MUCH TIME YOU SPEND IN A SHOPPING STATE OF MIND

Reading style blogs, fashion magazines, catalogs, and browsing *Pinterest* are fun, but they can make nice-to-have items feel like something you *have* to have. Curate your consumer-based media so that you're not spending time in an acquisitive mindset on a daily basis.

CULL YOUR EMAIL NEWSLETTERS

Most email newsletters amount to dressed-up invitations to go shopping—each and every time you open your inbox. It not only distracts you from more important tasks, but it also perpetually keeps you in a state where you're thinking about acquiring more things. Every four to six weeks, go on an "unsubscribe" spree to keep your inbox manageable and your temptation lowered.

☐ CHOOSE MORE THOUGHTFUL GIFTS

Giving a gift is such a nice thing, but the truth is that most gifts just get added to a pile of stuff that's rarely used. In order to give presents that are more of a match to the recipient, research has found that a gift is more appreciated if it's something the recipient would actually buy for herself—perhaps even something she's explicitly asked for—and that is easy for her to use (as opposed to overly complex or inconvenient). Or, instead of a more traditional present, consider giving food, plants, or donations in the recipient's name—they are all thoughtful, creative, and meaningful ways to show another person that you're thinking of them.

☐ ASSESS THE VALUE OF THE THINGS YOU DECIDE TO KEEP

If there's an item you're holding on to because you perceive it to be too valuable to let go, keep in mind that things are only worth what someone is willing to pay. An appraisal can go a long way toward helping you decide what's worth holding on to and what's not. If you want a more DIY option, check prices of similar items on *eBay* or other auction and resale websites.

KNOW YOURSELF

When deciding what to keep and what to let go, be honest with yourself. For example, if you aren't a baker, you don't need four pie plates. If there's an item you're not sure what to do with, ask yourself whether you're truly the kind of person who will put it to good use. If the answer is no, get that item to someone who will, and feel that much better about your home and yourself!

ADAPT TO YOUR SURROUNDINGS

If you just moved to the city, do you still need your car? If you moved to the country, do you still need your stiletto collection? Lining up your possessions with your life is a relief—it may seem like you're closing the door on possibility, but what you're actually doing is accepting where you are right now. If "one day" does come and you want the thing you've let go of, you can easily replace it—and if you do, you'll likely pick a product with a better fit for your new life. But odds are you never will.

RECOGNIZE HOW MUCH YOU ALREADY HAVE

To get better perspective on your stuff—and whether you need more of it—it helps to appreciate what you already have: the four walls and a roof that you call home, the bed that allows you to rest, the clothes that cover you up and express your style, the computer and cell phone that keep you connected, the food on the shelves that nourish you, and so on. Anything you can't muster any gratitude for probably needs to go to someone who can appreciate it.

DON'T EXPECT "ONE AND DONE"

A good decluttering session can make you feel lighter and more energized and is a great way to spend a Saturday afternoon, but it doesn't stop new things from making their way into your home. Acknowledging that decluttering is a process that you'll need to repeat at least once or twice a year helps you do it regularly so that your overall stuff level stays manageable.

☐ STEM THE TIDE

To keep the flow of stuff into your home at a manageable level, develop a quick check-in process to do each time you're considering buying something new. Ask yourself: *Do I need it? Do I love it? Will I use it? Can I afford it?* If the answer's no to any of these questions—be honest!—save yourself the task of having to declutter it later, and leave it on the shelf.

☐ TAKE A SHOPPING VACATION

Some shopping is necessary, some is frivolous, and some is purely habitual. To help raise your awareness on your unconscious spending, commit to not buying any new nonfood item for one day a week—maybe Tuesday, because it's a workday, or a Sunday, because it aligns with the idea of taking a Sabbath and many stores are closed then too. If that's easy, make it longer—two days, or even an entire week. The idea isn't to deprive yourself, but to make the things you do buy more meaningful.

☐ TAKE A STUFF VACATION

Pack up your knickknacks, stacks of paperwork—make sure there aren't any bills or checks in there—and anything that lives in plain sight on your counters, tables, or shelves. Now put them away for thirty days. When you get around to unpacking them, ask yourself, *Did I miss them? Did I need them?* Weigh those answers against how it felt to live in a space without visual clutter. If you answer "no," consider letting them go.

☐ WRITE A WILL

Writing a will is daunting, which explains why seven out of ten Americans haven't done it. But you don't do it for you—you do it for your loved ones, so they don't have to endure an extensive and expensive legal process to settle your estate after you're gone. Also, writing a will forces you to think through some big questions—such as whom you trust to make wise decisions on your behalf, and who you want to take care of your kids. Finally, contemplating your mortality has a way of making you more present to your life. Here's to it!

About the Author

Kate Hanley is an author, yoga teacher, and personal development coach who helps busy people get clear on what matters to them. In addition to working one on one with clients, Kate teaches and speaks at companies and events large and small. She's been quoted in a range of publications, from *Harvard Business Review* and Fortune.com to *Allure* and *Seventeen*, and has appeared on the *Today* show, where she noticed seconds before the cameras started rolling that her sweater was on backward. Kate lives in Providence, Rhode Island, with her husband and two kids. Visit her at KateHanley.com or on *Twitter* at @KateHan.